AF091992

THE WINSOME WAY

'REDISCOVERING THE EXTRAORDINARY IN YOURSELF AND ALL AROUND YOU'

DAN SNELL

Copyright © 2019 Dan Snell

THE W I N S O M E WAY

All rights reserved. No part of this publication may be reproduced, distributed, or transmitted in any form or by any means, including photocopying, recording, or other electronic or mechanical methods, without the prior written permission of the publisher, except in the case of brief quotations embodied in critical reviews and certain other noncommercial uses permitted by copyright law. For permission requests, write to the publisher, addressed "Attention: Permissions Coordinator," at info@beyondpublishing.net

Quantity sales special discounts are available on quantity purchases by corporations, associations, and others. For details, contact the publisher at the address above.

Orders by U.S. trade bookstores and wholesalers. Email info@BeyondPublishing.net

The Beyond Publishing Speakers Bureau can bring authors to your live event. For more information or to book an event contact the Beyond Publishing Speakers Bureau speak@BeyondPublishing.net

The Author can be reached directly BeyondPublishing.net/AuthorDanSnell and TheWinsomeWay.com

Manufactured and printed in the United States of America distributed globally by BeyondPublishing.net

New York | Los Angeles | London | Sydney

Hardcover ISBN: 978-1-949873-99-3

Softcover ISBN: 978-1-949873-11-5

DEDICATION

This book I dedicate first to you, the reader
as The Winsome Way is a message about keeping your eye on 'others first'.

Most importantly I want to thank God for my wonderful parents,
L.D. and Kitty Snell, for sharing their hearts and passion for service.
Their ever-winsome spirit for people and community lives on.

With love and encouragement to Sarah,
Lee and Amanda to carry it forward,
alongside their spouses Craig for Sarah and Haley for Lee.
Amanda, my youngest, your special day for Dad
to walk you down the aisle will come in time.
Lastly and as they've lived less than 100 days here on earth as I write this,
I joyfully add to the dedication of this book, newborn grandchildren
Benjamin Craig and Winnie Lee.

ACKNOWLEDGEMENTS

I believe that every person has a book inside them waiting to come out. When they write it, they'll understand this quote that was read at the funeral of a young man I once coached in baseball, Kevin Sloup.

There is a destiny which makes us brothers; none goes his way alone. All that we send into the lives of others comes back into our own.

~ Edwin Markham

In that quote lies the reason to acknowledge so many people who have poured heart, love, support, encouragement, prayers and ideas into my life and the making of this book. Also, their positive ways of challenging me made me better. While acknowledgement pages may be skipped over by 98% of readers, each of these people below, and I'm sure many I missed that should be here, helped make Dan, the Dan who wrote the book.

To my two wonderful older yet still youthful sisters Janice and Judy. They put up with their little kid brother for so many years they laugh about it I'm sure. Their husbands Jim and Hugh respectively, and all their incredible children and grandchildren help keep my Mom and Dad's winsome legacy rolling.

My children, again. You are a gift from God. At times life handed us lemons and we worked to make lemonade. Remember that 'Attitude is Everything… keep yours Winsome!' You are my greatest accomplishment. Your best years are still to come. Serve your families. Serve your friends and community Somebody run for public office and keep a 150 years legacy of elective public service going.

Thankful for the Snell and Koke heritage of which cries out 'serve'! Special shout out to cousin Mike Ehlers for his prayers and encouragement always. And for finding genealogy that lives on.

To my publisher and newfound mentor, coach, friend and cheerleader Michael D. Butler. No words. This happened. You made it happen. I hope I can repay my gratitude.

To the Zig and Jean Ziglar Family. Julie, Tom and Cindy, the amazing legacy of Zig and Jean. And the late Jim Norman, Julie's amazing giant hearted husband. And Bryan Flanagan, Bob Beaudine, Michael Kennedy and Lauri Magers who I met through the

Ziglar clan. Your friendship, support, kindness and foremost your continuation of your Dad's legacy holds my highest admiration. This book would not have been written if not for your Dad's words *'you got some good ideas up there in that enthusiastic brain of yours, young man. Write the book!'* I know Jean and Zig see it now.

Thanks to so many I've worked with professionally over the years. Wow! I learned so much from you! We won battles together, climbed business mountains together, suffered losses together, celebrated President's Clubs and awards together. Aron Ain, Mike McNiel, Bruce Bell, Jeff West, Ken Hanaway, Tammy Helton, Mike Traw, Jay Wreidt, Dorine Olive, Curtis Criss, Gene 'Lageman' Lage, Philip Seeger, Jerry Jaskowiak, Bruce Bartmann, Dean 'Gutz' Gutzke, Kerry Wicks, Gary Loflin, Greg Hannah, Tiffany VanDeBerg, Brian Denomme, Mike Knocke, Mike Debus, Matt Knight, Dave and Barb Pitcock, Gigi Belmonico, James Malinchak, Christopher and Tara Borghese. Daryl Miller. I'm sure there are so many more I missed.

To the City of Shawnee KS, where it was my honor to serve 5 terms, particularly to former City Manager Gary Montague, and the late mentors and friends Roy D. Shenkel, Rob Roberts and Joe Mayo, we accomplished much together. Many media friends so numerous to list but they know their names. I remember all. And so many great Councilmembers and Mayors I served with in 10 years of office.

To other mentors and friends in Public Service. Mayor Rich Becker, State Senator Gus Bogina, his son and my campaign champion, Augie Bogina, Bill Nicks, Jr., Rick Hoffman, Gary Blumenthal, General Phill Kline, Jim Allen, Don Opplinger, Jeff Meyers and more.

To Pastors and people I've served others with out in the faith community. Jimmy Dodd, Carey Casey, Ken Monroe, Trace Thurlby, Dick and Rich Bott, Leon & Renee Patillo, Vince D'Acchioli, JJ Jasper, Jonathan Wright, Craig Miller, Kerry Maire Godfrey, the late Dan Erickson, Dr. Randy Shepard, Bill Byington, Russ & Jackie Jones, Curtis Criss, Dan Woglemuth, Chris Pinion, Rupert James Sr., Rick Lindsey, Gary Johnson, Bob Hodgdon, "Robman" Kannard, Wilson Metz, Rick Lindsay, Danny Duran, Tim and Ellen Swartz, Kerry Godfrey and so many more.

For some special people who prayed, supported and inspired me while in the valley during tough times; Jim and Mary Odom, Jim and Debbie Collier, Dr. George Stamos, Doug Hood, Dr Ken Canfield, Bob Sherwood, Doug Bachtel, Dr. Randy Shepard, Dr George Stamos, James Malinchak, Kristy Orison, Doug Hood, Coach Tony Brown, Sheryl Dillard, Penelope Cain, Rick and Janelle Grimes, Jesse Hall, Curt and Melinda Houdyshell, Mike Yardley, Jesse Hall, Don Collins, Marsha Anderson and Darcee Lynn Juel.

To those in and around my life of loving, playing, coaching and refereeing sports. Dale Kerkman, Ross Ridenour, Fr. Bob Roh, Pat Behrns, Doug Miller, Jesse Hall, who got me my NBA refereeing shot, John McCarthy, Rick Waggener, Paul Coffman, Chris and Heather Creighton, Willie Cashmore, Pat Williams, Mike Moore, the Smith basketball family, as well as the school systems my children played and excelled in sports in. Drake University holds a special place and made me an NCAA photographer. Special kudos to the late and enthusiastic Husker sportscaster Lyle Bremser for instilling the 'Go Big Red' spirit about all things we believe in.

To all my Nebraska friends, high school and college pals and life memories; Greg Scholz, Dale Dolezal, Dave Kozisek, Mike Armstrong, Dan Roh, Rich and Mary Gillespie, Rick Grubaugh, John Kopecky, Larry 'Bernie' Austin, the entire Dehner, Vanous, Forester, Hottovy and Trowbridge families; my former high school sweetheart Luann and the Moravec family, Gary Novotny, Tom Henning, the late Ron VanMeter, Steve Tines, Robert Fitzgerald, Larry and Lauriann Scott, Phi Chapter of TKE, Aquinas Class of 1974, Aquinas Alumni and UNL Alumni Associations.

Some exceptional encouragers of the last three years that I'd like to give shout outs: Sheriff Mark Owen, Deputy Sheriff Erik Holland, Chief Rob Groseclose, Sgt. Dylan Wilson, 911 Director Carole Moreland, Chief Clint Reno, Lt. Larry Tarrant, Chief Rich Lockhart, Chief Bob Muenz, Dan Hood, Capt. Rea Myers, Det. James Brock, Sheriff Paul Filla, Deputy Sheriff Chris Martin and many others in the law enforcement community.

And with a thankful heart for Rebecca and Molliann.

THE IDEAL PROFESSIONAL SPEAKER FOR YOUR NEXT EVENT!

Any organization that wants to DEVELOP, ENCOURAGE and INSPIRE their people to discover the EXTRAORDINARY in themselves, their teams and for their future, needs to hire Dan for a <u>keynote message</u> or <u>workshop training</u>.
Dan personally works closely in the planning and preparation, adding value to your event.

Associations
Corporate
Sales Kickoffs
Sales Training
Sports Banquets
Athletic Programs
Churches
Non-Profits
Community Banquets

TO CONTACT OR BOOK DAN TODAY TO SPEAK:

The Winsome Way

913-908-8175

Dan@TheWinsomeWay.com

www.TheWinsomeWay.com

@TheWinsomeWay

Do you have a book, a message or story, or even a film script inside you that you want to explore bringing forth to the world?

Michael D. Butler at Beyond Publishing has helped hundreds of authors, speakers and film production teams bring their message and magic to millions across the globe.

The differences and benefits in using a 'hybrid publisher' are many and are the reason why so many are turning to the Beyond Publishing team. Find out why your book may be closer than you think!

For more information and learn how Michael Butler has helped authors, *just like Dan Snell and this book*, bring their message and talent to millions across the world, contact Michael today at:

Michael@BeyondPublishing.net

www.BeyondPublishing.net

TABLE OF CONTENTS

Foreword 13
Introduction 17
Chapter 1 Defining Winsome 27
The Winsome Acronym 33

Chapter 2 The "W" for Willing 43
Three Winsome Presidents 45
   John Fitzgerald Kennedy – Winsome Presence, Winsome Statesman 45
   Ronald Reagan – President and Inspiration 49
   William Jefferson Clinton 51
   The Serial CEO – Tom Henning 52

Chapter 3 The "I" for Interested 55
   The Mission is ReMission – Pat Williams 60
   Winsome and Smart - Robert J. Sherwood 61
   Social Chairman - CPA - Pastor Larry Austin, Jr. 64

Chapter 4 The " N" for Nurturing 67
   Dr. Dan Erickson - Ever Nurturing Trademark Phrase 71
   The Kindergarten Bus Driver - Bob 'Mr. Donut' Donner 72
   Three Winsome Women 74
   The Nun 74
   The Cook 75
   The Queen 76

Chapter 5 The "S" for 'Solutioneering' 79
   You Always Remember Your First Sale – Bob Balderston 84
   The Positivity Guy - Michael C. Saubert, Sr. 84
   Secret Millionaire and Consummate Solutioneer - James Malinchak 85

Chapter 6 The "O" for Optimism 87
  Gas Station Attendant Millionaire – Larry Scott 85
  Small Town USA Leadership – Greg Scholz 93

Chapter 7 The "M" for Mindful 99
  The Milkman - Bill Eller 108
  The Zig Ziglar of UNL – Dr. Keith Pritchard 110

Chapter 8 The "E" for Enroller 113
  Style and Enthusiasm - Gary Novotny 117
  America's Mayor – Rich Becker 120

Chapter 9 Five Winsome Companies 125

Chapter 10 The Winsome Seven 131

Chapter 11 - Winsome Coaching 143

FOREWORD

BY TOM ZIGLAR

Being the "Proud Son" of Zig Ziglar, and now working daily and to carry on my Dad's legacy, I've met and worked with hundreds of incredible people. Dan Snell, author of this book "The Winsome Way" is one such person. The pages ahead are an extension of Ziglar inspiration to others that was my Dad's heart and soul.

I remember that 2010 morning phone call when an enthusiastic voice on the other end of the line wanted to talk about Dad's book, "Raising Positive Kids in a Negative World". It was Dan Snell. We did not know each other at all. He called with gusto and a winsome smile that came across through the phone lines. I now reflect that was the beginning of our 'winsome friendship'. He called asking if Dad might be able to be on a Sunday morning radio program for blended families that Dan was co-hosting.

Dan shared the story of first meeting Dad in St Louis, MO in a Sheraton Hotel lobby during a Get Motivated event Dad was speaking at. I could 'feel' the story as if I was there. We connected also that day in talking about how we both were blessed by our respective Dad's, who led lives focused on serving others. My sister Julie and I, along with her husband Jim, ended up on that Sunday radio program and talked about 'Growing Up Ziglar' and how positive parenting can make a difference, even in a stepfamily environment. My Dad, and Jim, are now both in Heaven, yet they echo into eternity even in the Foreword for this book. I later spoke at a fundraising luncheon for Dan and that was my first 'paid' engagement as a speaker.

The energy, faith and devotion toward serving others that I have witnessed in Dan in our last decade of knowing one another, continues in this book THE WINSOME WAY. Dan is living testimony to his message. He shares in this quick and fun read about 'walking winsome through life' and how will open doors, build relationships and foster wonderful surprises and greater success in every aspect of life, family and business.

It was Dan's winsome 'be willing' approach that led him to approach my Dad that day in St Louis in 1999 and start a friendship which would eventually lead Dad inspiring Dan to write this book. And now, for me, 20 years later, writing this Foreword brings a smile via a 20 year 'encouragement legacy' I'm able to extend.

As I write this, I share that the very word 'foreword' means 'to come before'. In this book you will not only read a breakdown and acronym of the word 'W-I-N-S-O-M-E but you will hear stories of how many encouraging and 'winsome' people, including Dan's Dad and my Dad, came before and poured into Dan's life, impacted him in a special way to help shape a positive, upbeat, cheerful and 'always look for the good' spirit we see encouraged in this book as the way to 'discover the extraordinary in others'.

In the book you will find the acronym:

      W = Be Willing
       I = Be Interested
      N = Be a Nurturer
       S = Be a Solutioneer
      O = Be Optimistic
      M = Be Mindful
      E = Be an Enroller

All these qualities are ones that me to share with enthusiasm that Dan in his own words shares the Zig Ziglar foundational philosophy that 'You can have everything you want in life, if you just help enough other people get what they want'. Enjoy this book go discover the best and brightest in those around you.

With Best Regards

Tom Ziglar, *Proud Son of Zig Ziglar*

THE WINSOME WAY

INTRODUCTION

Live your day the WINSOME Way! Your WINSOME WALK begins NOW, as you've picked up this book.

You've opened this book to discover a new and exciting place to go. Perhaps you are 'hungry' for something different than you know. For a life different then you've been living. You're not alone. A Gallup poll recently found that over 74 percent of Americans were not happy at their job and that less that 15 percent felt 'engaged' in their workplace. Isn't that a sad statistic? The Winsome Way offers you a daily path, a daily action plan to have you become more engaged in your world, so you can live each and every day… the WINSOME Way!

Since somewhere around 1998, Americans have been on a roller coaster of emotions, finances, feelings of safety and security, and foremost, the wonder if we can hold hope for a better future and the American Dream.

We walked through so many new experiences in these last 20 years. We experienced an unprecedented positive economy in the 90s. Personally, it was one of the top two decades of my sales career.

The period from 1991 to 2001 was the was the longest economic expansion in the history of the United States. If you remember what business you were in, generally it was good. I was in the technology arena, and it was go-go, sell-sell, double digit growth after double digit growth. The era called the 'Dot Com Bubble' had created high-energy financial growth and a host of new names and entrepreneurs galore.

401(k)'s rose strongly, along with the stock market. Job creation was estimated at over 23 million new jobs. In a true and even bigger part of life, America was experiencing a rebirth of patriotism with love of country and respect for the military seemingly high. We were a strong nation again with a charismatic 'winsome' leader in President Bill Clinton. (More on the winsome nature of Clinton later in book.) In the technology world, we were, as they say, 'kicking butt and taking names'. Sales were tremendous.

Then… that brings you and I to one of the reasons this book was written. We saw and lived out a true roller coaster ride that began as we began a new century. Our foundation as a nation, as individuals, as families and in our ability to feel good about ourselves and our future began to change. The economy slowly started to become weary in 1999. A 'created fear' of the turn of the century, called 'Y2K', set forth uncertainty as to 'what will happen to all computers, financial markets, infrastructure, and technology that depended on a 'clock' internally'. Personally, I loved it. I produced revenue of over four million dollars in the software industry providing 'solutions' to ease those fears.

The economy began to stumble. Growth and/or hope of growth faltered. The stock market took serious downward trends and dives. The Federal Reserve hiked interest rates.

We saw the true lack of leadership from Washington's political climate. The ideas of elected officials working together for the nation's good left us. That Washington brokenness has become today sadly our leading arena of 'woesome' behavior from both parties. Working for their own specific agendas became the norm. We saw our capitol become a place that no longer fosters leadership and unity, but instead, became a place of negativity and a 'make wrong machine' style that shouts, 'they have to be really bad so I can be good'.

Then…BOOM… September 11th, 2001, known forever as simply "9-11" struck our nation. Terrorism came to the shores of America. Next to President John F. Kennedy's assassination or the space shuttle explosion, it has become the single most 'where were you when…' question in the last 50 years.

The World Trade Center's twin towers crumbled before our eyes on national TV. We experienced fear, uncertainty, doubt, anger, agony, and loss. We became a people with questions. A nation wanting to know who, what, how, why, and what will we do next, or what might happen next.

I believe President George Bush was clearly the person 'for such a time as this' and led with steady, firm resolve. He appeared presidential in his compassion, authority, and resolute determination. His message to the world was firm and clear. It is still much too soon to determine if his responses and actions were the right ones. It is always easy to question the most powerful office in the land. If you've faced crisis or similar scenarios, you understand. I've always encouraged people to 'get the facts' and hold one's negative attacks on leadership until the smoke has cleared. In 9-11's case, we may not fully know as a nation for many years.

Generally, these last 18+ years birthed a season of feeling a little lost. Do you know what I mean? From a national confidence level, we never really fully recovered. Did you, yourself, walk on some of those unsteady roads in your life? Do you agree with me that as a nation, and as individuals, it's time for a comeback? I believe it is a time for special surge of walking winsome. That's why I wrote this book, and you and I are together on this winsome journey. To renew the American Spirit. To lift up and encourage people. Foremost, encourage just one person this moment, and that is YOU, to believe in yourself and what you can do, to treat others as you would like to be treated, and to hold in your heart, mind, and soul the powerful characteristics and lessons of THE WINSOME WAY.

The Winsome Way is somewhere between a fearless boldness, the desire to improve one's life, and that unique ever-living spirit in each of us to try to become what you could be. And foremost being an outward-bound encouragement to others. You will find this book to be 'others-focused'

> So, let's do this together! Okay? We can do this! Speak the words out loud boldly and with a smile,
> # "I CAN DO THIS!"
> **BELIEVE IT!**

If you're holding this book in your hands this moment, I suggest to you that you will never be the same. The winsome concepts, ideas, tips, coaching, and methods will have a measurable impact on your life. And within 10 days. Yes, this can and *will* happen fast! Every day counts! Is that what you want? Change…fast? You'll discover quickly and grow as you walk through a 10-day journey toward your winsome life. This book is in your hands perhaps because of several reasons. All of them good! BELIEVE they are good, read this book looking for good, and our time together will lead to the best days of your life that are just ahead!

You may be holding this book in your hand because:

- You are searching for a better way to connect to people.
- You just lost your job or failed in a relationship, and you're thinking, *There must be a better way*.
- A manager handed you this book and said, "Read and grow winsome, grow mighty."
- A friend or relative (an exceptionally smart person!) gave you this book to 'change your life'.
- You may be someone with your eyes always glued to your cell phone and know there's a better way.
- You're in a small group study for church, community, book club, business, etc.
- You heard that on average, winsome people earn 10 percent more than the average person.
- You heard research shows being winsome adds seven years to your life.

- You want some of that joy, positivity, and energy, and you heard me on one of my broadcasts.
- We just met at an event, the airport, a restaurant, or coffee shop, and we connected.
- You heard about this 'winsome' trend sweeping the country and wanted to live the 'Winsome Way'.
- Your marriage or family is struggling, and you're looking for a different approach.
- You're in the bookstore, and BOOM, *The Winsome Way* jumped off the shelf and into your hands.
- You are sitting in an audience and I'm speaking on the stage at your event (let me sign your book!).

Whatever the scenario, your best life is ahead! Now, please do this. It's STEP ONE to a breakthrough, and I ask you to let go of your inhibitions to be able to express joy and excitement and have some simple fun.

So here we start! Stop, set this book down for just a moment, look around, nodding and smiling at those around you and say boldly three times out loud…

HOORAY! TODAY I START BEING WINSOME!

Imagine you are somewhere where your words will echo. Think of your words actually echoing back to you in a canyon or a great arena! People may smile back and ask, "Hey, what are you reading there?"

Celebrate yourself this moment. Celebrate that you are undertaking a personal development plan that will improve your life! There is something in each of us that says, "Reach." Something that says, "I have a dream." Listen to that voice! The Creator of the Universe made you special. He's in each of us. Our purpose. You have developed special talents in your life, and it's time to shine brighter than ever! Let's go find it together!

Our society often refuses to show joy or excitement or enthusiasm when we should truly feel it. It's okay to be happy and excited. We often measure too heavily lesser or negative moments that pop up via social media —Facebook, Instagram, SnapChat, Twitter, or other sites — when it's best left less celebrated. Yet when it's personal, real, and in the moment, we don't fully celebrate the moment.

Throughout the book, you'll discover 'WINSOME-ISMS' that might become set points, key memory makers, or concepts that truly stick with you as you walk forward winsome.

One such 'WINSOME-ISM" is the three-letter acronym, WCM, which stands for "Winsome Celebration Moments". Which means why not celebrate and enjoy and living life big! Too often, we do not celebrate victorious moments, big or small. Inside, we feel it, but something says don't show your excitement – and I say tell that voice to jump in the lake. Like right now. Stand up again and say, "I'm going places, and I'm walking winsome all the way there!" Celebrate yourself on this journey! We intend to walk winsome like we should, and we will thrive and shine once we fully get the winsome way planted in our heart.

Look back at this last week. If you, your family, your friend, your spouse, or someone close to you 'won the moment'… did you do stand up, smile, speak, and celebrate? Right now, you are reading this book and, perhaps, wanting a breakthrough from the too often negative shackles of society. Research shows only about two in ten will truly speak positive words aloud. Those other eight – and I believe you are not a part of them, as you're reading this book - are conditioned to lock down and bridle their enthusiasm for happiness or even a big moment.

A big-time challenge in our society today is a lack of gusto for what we do. There tends to be a cynicism about all things enthusiastic. Often, a lack of teamwork and caring for others is the norm. A self-centered or self-interested focus — what I call 'cubicle thinking'— has a grip on people. The 'me, myself, and I' world has been fostered in many circles.

In his outstanding series of books on optimism, Dr. Martin E.P. Seligman writes of the epidemic of pessimism in America. Of depression and discouragement. He notes that we ignore the damage of suicide to families and society. That more people die each year from suicide than from AIDS. I join the quest and the spirit of Dr. Seligman to transform society and help people understand and get engaged in 'learning' both optimism and a winsome way of life. The message of the Winsome Way is not new. It is as timeless as people following an encouraging word, a persevering spirit, an inspirational message, and yes, now, a winsome way.

Jesus Christ, Gandhi, Teddy Roosevelt, Eleanor Roosevelt, John F. Kennedy, Mother Teresa, Jackie Robinson, Joe Namath, Willie Mays, Muhammad Ali, Ronald Reagan, Bill Clinton, Barack Obama, and current personalities, like Dwayne "The Rock" Johnson and Ellen DeGeneres. These very special people all walked— or still walk— with a special winsome quality that drew people to them.

In 1882, a writer named Richard Glover wrote a book entitled *Winsome Christianity*. As a man who strives daily to be a person of faith, I believe that people can and *should* be able to walk with a winsome manner when it comes to their core beliefs. The Bible is a book that offers true hope, guidance, inspiration, and opportunity. If we trust the precepts, we'd live more winsomely. It can add to the positivity we carry in life.

Over 70 years ago, Henry Durbanville wrote his own version of the same title, *Winsome Christianity*. In Durbanville's version, he spoke of Jesus being "the most winsome man ever". That even his enemies were drawn to Him. Jesus, of course, had some supernatural powers given to Him by his heavenly Father, yet we can learn much from his walk while he was on the earth.

Since that period of Christ over 2,000 years ago, we slowly have grown more and more the tendency to fear and not share trust in others. People often don't want to admit that. We are cautious to touch or be touched physically or emotionally. The self-focused world we live in today has seen a tendency toward a disinterest to reach out, step up, serve our neighbor, be a team or community leader or volunteer. We even shy away from speaking an encouraging or positive word to another, lest someone think we're wanting something, or the compliment isn't real. We've developed a nation of naysayers, doubters, social media bashers, and quiet poop throwers.

This book, not unlike other books seeks to impact a generation and beyond. My genuine hope is something you read will allow you to gather 'breakthrough boldness' tips and powerful ways to express yourself for the good of all and walk through life in a winsome way.

This book also is intended especially for YOU to be a LOOK BACK and SAY THANKS book. In each chapter, I will highlight the lives of some wonderful people who impacted my life. All winsome people. People who poured themselves in some way or another and impacted my life. NOW TO YOU and those in your life who you could say were 'WINSOME'.

Pause. Think on your list right now before you continue to read. Write down their names below. And now as an important note to you: reach out to your list. Call them. Email them. FaceTime them. Whatever is available. If they are deceased, call their spouse, or even their children. Say thank you! Recall what they did. Your 'winsome' memories of these people from your own childhood and growing up will be like visiting with them in person. As you let them know that you thought of them and wanted to say thanks, suddenly you're on your way to your winsome life. You're putting others as the focus. Somebody's day – that winsome person you wish to honor - will be impacted. Set this book aside now, and write down the names of your winsome impact people. Try to reach at least one right now. WATCH WHAT IT DOES FOR THEM. BUT BIGGER…WATCH WHAT IT DOES FOR YOU!

My Winsome Mentors / Life Inventory – Who 'Touched' Me The Most

(Don't worry about the order—just the first people who come to your mind. Then, rank them 1-10.)

_____	1 2 3 4 5 6 7 8 9 10
_____	1 2 3 4 5 6 7 8 9 10
_____	1 2 3 4 5 6 7 8 9 10
_____	1 2 3 4 5 6 7 8 9 10
_____	1 2 3 4 5 6 7 8 9 10
_____	1 2 3 4 5 6 7 8 9 10
_____	1 2 3 4 5 6 7 8 9 10
_____	1 2 3 4 5 6 7 8 9 10
_____	1 2 3 4 5 6 7 8 9 10
_____	1 2 3 4 5 6 7 8 9 10

The concepts of 'The Winsome Way' are gleaned from years of being a student of the giants in motivation, inspiration, leadership, and encouragement. People like Zig Ziglar, Jim Rohn, W. Clement Stone,

Dale Carnegie, Napoleon Hill, Tony Robbins, Joel Osteen, Louise Hay, Les Brown, Mel Robbins, Eric Thomas, Brendon Burchard, and others. While I lay no claims to standing alongside these giants of positivity and inspiration in any way, there is, without a doubt, an 'enthusiasm deficit' in our world today. 'The Winsome Way' offers ideas that you can use to grow your family life, business success, spiritual depth, and even physical strength and longevity.

You will set this book down and have a tendency to often cite and talk about the concepts—especially one of the seven (WINSOME) acronym letters and their meaning—as you walk through your daily life. And with that… you will begin to live each day THE WINSOME WAY.

CHAPTER 1
DEFINING WINSOME

If you reach for the Webster's Dictionary, or simply tap the keyboard on your computer, tablet, or smartphone, you can look up the meaning of the word 'winsome'.

You'll find the following via Dictionary.com / Merriam-Webster

cheerful, upbeat, happy, energetic, youthful or innocent charm; winning;

engaging: a winsome smile

If this be WINSOME… wouldn't you want to BE WINSOME?

> **Check out this list of Synonyms:**
>
> *absorbing, alluring, appealing, attractive, captivating, pretty, sweet, charismatic, delightful, desirable, elegant, enamoring, engaging, enthralling, eye-catching, fascinating, glamorous, inviting, irresistible, lovable, pleasant, pleasing, hopeful, optimistic, gladsome, perky, upbeat, good-humored, good-natured, peppy, zippy, winning*

Re-read that definition and the synonyms. I would guess that 95 percent of the people reading those would like to BE those. And the other five percent are liars. They make movies about grinches. Yet in the end, even the Grinch turns his heart to goodness.

You'll often hear me say, "Be winsome and be victorious! Walk winsome and walk victorious!"

In my study and years of personal research of winsome people, I have found they easily win friends, and win in the moment, so it is not surprising that *winsome* and *win* have a common root. Their shared element, win-, comes from the Indo-European root *wen-, meaning "to desire, strive for." Another is the Germanic noun *wini-, meaning "friend" (literally, "one who desires or loves" someone else). A different form of the root with a different suffix became Old English wynn, "pleasure, joy," preserved in winsome. So, for yourself, your family, your friends, and your business world, remember to carry with you the lessons that you will glean from THE WINSOME WAY.

If you remember just one point in the meaning or root analysis of the word winsome, remember that the verb WIN, itself, is from this root; its meaning is an extension of the sense "to strive for," namely "to strive for with success, be victorious."

In Proverbs 15:13-15, the Bible offers some profound wisdom – as it always does – when it speaks to a cheerful and joyful heart.

> *A joyful heart makes a cheerful face, but when the heart is sad, the spirit is broken. The mind of the intelligent seeks knowledge, but the mouth of fools feeds on folly. All the days of the afflicted are bad, but a cheerful heart has a continual feast.*
>
> Proverbs 15: 13-15

A Continual feast? Wow! Did you hear that? That's a promise, not a suggestion. That's a heavenly message of truth for YOU! Let's start feasting on a new and winsome way of life!

In my study of successful people, I've rarely come across people who like to lose. I've met few who accept defeat easily and walk away. That's not to say true champions do not learn from their defeats and use them to get stronger and better at what they do, yet they do *not* like to lose. They, indeed, enter the arena seeking to win. Being your best helps you 'walk winsome'.

Sometimes in life, you get on a roll. Everything seems to be going your way. You find a perfect job, then find an awesome match for a spouse, and then the first home dream comes true. The money starts rolling in, and you're able to travel and purchase your wishes and wants and the things you've dreamed of. Then… BOOM…something happens. Like momentum shifting in a football game, things start to go against you. 'Turnovers' happen. There's competition that has risen up. Your boss starts having stinkin' thinkin' about you. Sales are off. Productivity drops. Your relationships are souring. Cash flow is tight. You're not feeling good about life. What is happening?!? Suddenly, things are going downhill. We'll refer to that in future chapters as 'Needing a Win'. Sometimes a "W" during the downward momentum can reboot your success. I often speak of and post on social media pictures of me buying a "W" and posting 'sometimes you just need a "W". People get it. Sometimes we are just down and need a little win. A "W"!

The legendary Washington Redskins football coach George Allen was once quoted as saying, "When you lose, you die a thousand deaths, but then, when you win, you're born again." Win starts with "W". Winsome starts with "W". Being Winsome leads to more "W's". Let's go get some "W's"!

You may be reading this and get that automatically. I know that there will be someone reading who perhaps has tasted a number of losses and are finding it tough to rise up again. To those readers, I say, "Great! Glad you have this book in hand! Let's go get a 'W'." You've won before. You will win again. And you will do so more consistently if you follow the precepts of this book.

For every one of my children, for every team I've ever coached, and for every individual I've managed or mentored, they know what I'm about to say. They've heard me say it 100 times as I worked to instill it into the fabric of their being. Words have power! Words can start, end, or win a war. Let there be no mistake that these words mean everything to success in any endeavor. Repeat this out loud three times now and daily.

Zig Ziglar: The Embodiment of Winsome

> *"You can have everything you want in life, if you just help enough other people get what they want."*
>
> *~ Zig Ziglar*

I remember driving in my car on a late November 2012 Friday afternoon listening to Zig Ziglar on a CD. It was a four-hour drive back from St. Louis to Kansas City. Zig would always say to "use that windshield time to learn"—almost like a university, he would say. The following Wednesday, we learned of his death. I reflected back on that Friday drive, thinking, *Gosh, I was just listening to him. Zig would be proud of me.* Listening to motivational and inspirational tapes like Zig and others would help make anyone winsome for sure. And to honor Zig, I, too, encourage you to enroll in 'Windshield University'.

> *"Attitude is Everything!"*

This quote has been attributed to many: W. Clement Stone, Zig Ziglar, Dr. Wayne Dyer, Charles Stanley, Chuck Swindoll, and others. Research claims the original author of this tremendous quote is 'Unknown'. Whomever it is and whoever claims it, it's okay, because it's the message that 'attitude is everything' that really matters, and you should remember your attitude impacts your winsome way.

On the subject of 'who said it', let me share a smile with you that Zig Ziglar told me in our very first meeting in the green room at a Get Motivated seminar in Springfield, Missouri, in October of 2009. I was sharing with Zig the years of sales success I'd been blessed with, and part of that success came from using his quotes. Being the man of integrity and joyful wit always, Zig shared that he didn't originate all of his quotes, that many he picked up from reading books (Zig read three hours daily) and listening to great speakers and leaders. He winked and smiled and shared, "When I use a great quote, phrase, or story the first few times, I always give credit to whom it came from. After a dozen or so references, I say, 'I once heard a true legendary wise man say...' After about the 20th time I share it, I just say, 'I often say...'" Zig gave the originator the credit in appropriate fashion, whether speaking or in his books, and after that, it became part of his messages, too, so he was free to borrow.

Throughout *The Winsome Way*, you'll see quotes and inspirations from Zig Ziglar. Meeting him, having some special photographic memories with him (see photo chapter) was a true thrill. The little boy excitement came out in me, even though I had reached what I called 'The Age of Distinction', 50 years old. If you're over 50, you know you're still young, just seasoned. If your 50s are a long way off and you think 50 is old, I'm smiling and encouraging that the best is still to come. Stay tuned!

The Reverend Chuck Swindoll, who I had the pleasure of meeting during my time as a radio executive with the Bott Radio Network, once published the following brief commentary, often called his poem, on attitude. It, too, has become a frequently referred to 'attitude' development message. If you haven't seen this, I suggest copying, scanning, taking a picture and putting it on your Facebook, Twitter, Instagram—or even better, do it the old-fashioned way of writing it down and carrying it all folded up in your billfold. The following script on the next page, written by the Rev. Chuck Swindoll, is worth sharing with your friends, family, and all.

> ### *Attitude*
>
> *The longer I live, the more I realize the impact of attitude on life.*
>
> *Attitude, to me, is more important than facts. It is more important than the past, than education, than money, than circumstances, than failure, than successes, than what other people think or say or do. It is more important than appearance, giftedness, or skill. It will make or break a company... a church... a home.*
>
> *The remarkable thing is we have a choice everyday regarding the attitude we will embrace for that day. We cannot change our past...we cannot change the fact that people will act in a certain way. We cannot change the inevitable.*
>
> *The only thing we can do is play on the one string we have, and that is our attitude. I am convinced that life is 10 percent what happens to me and 90 percent how I react to it.*
>
> *~ Rev. Chuck Swindoll*

Even today, in his 70s, Rev. Chuck Swindoll continues to be a bright light of attitude and inspiration daily to me and to thousands with his daily email messages.

And of course, from one of the inspirations of this book and the undisputed champion of modern-day attitude, motivation, and inspiration:

> *Positive thinking won't let you do anything, but it will let you do everything better than negative thinking will.*
>
> ~ Zig Ziglar

Read on to learn some of the great attitudes I've been fortunate to be around in my life.

THE

ACRONYM

Because a Winsome spirit and life is a living and breathing action, we start with a "be…"

W = be Willing

I = be Interested

N = be Nurturing

S = be a "Solutioneer"

O = be Optimistic

M = be Mindful

E = be an Enroller

Walk Winsome.

Be Winsome.

Live Winsome.

Win Winsome.

"The Winsome Champions in Your Life"

"YAWYAW" -- You Are Who You Associate With"

My friend, Bob Beaudine, is a nationally recognized motivational speaker and author I'll mention often in this book. Bob wrote *The Power of Who*, and he first shared with me the YAWYAW phrase. Discussing successful business relationships over lunch in Plano, Texas, he acknowledged that he didn't originate 'YAWYAW', but believed in it in his own life. (Remember my Zig Ziglar story about giving credit for sayings a few times? So I credit Bob now here, and later I won't. Ha! Just kidding, Bobby!)

YAWYAW means "You Are Who You Associate With". We are absolutely the collective mixture of those we associate with, and it stems from the first days of our lives to this very day. We tend to become like the friends and close ones we are most connected to. I believe our income, our personality, our marriages or relationships, our faith, and our character are all reflected back by the seven people we are closest to. We'll speak of the 'Winsome Seven' concept later in the book, and it will help create in you the winsomeness you seek.

In Proverbs 13:20, the Bible shares,

> *'He who walks with wise men will be wise, but the companion of fools will suffer harm.'*

Written a long time ago, but still right on target today. I know. Like my friend Bob, who I love to spend time with, those who we are closest to impact us the most. Our spouse. Our co-workers. Our family. Our old high school or college buddies, church friends, neighbors, social clubs, or even Mastermind groups, etc.

So, let's take an inventory of those who are impacting your thinking. They 'touch' you with encouragement and optimism, or they 'touch' you with negativity or pessimism. After you list them, to the right, give them a scale of 1 to 10 positivity factor. Later, we'll discuss their winsome factor to see if they might become part of your 'Winsome Seven'. Plug into the line following a quick inventory of those YAWYAW people in your life.

My Close People Inventory – Who 'Touches' Me The Most

(don't worry about order or ranking, just the first people who come to mind)

My Winsome Seven List

Name	Rating
_____	1 2 3 4 5 6 7 8 9 10
_____	1 2 3 4 5 6 7 8 9 10
_____	1 2 3 4 5 6 7 8 9 10
_____	1 2 3 4 5 6 7 8 9 10
_____	1 2 3 4 5 6 7 8 9 10
_____	1 2 3 4 5 6 7 8 9 10
_____	1 2 3 4 5 6 7 8 9 10
_____	1 2 3 4 5 6 7 8 9 10
_____	1 2 3 4 5 6 7 8 9 10
_____	1 2 3 4 5 6 7 8 9 10
_____	1 2 3 4 5 6 7 8 9 10

Bob Beaudine had terrific parents. His father, Frank Beaudine, was a giant mentor in his business and personal life. Bob speaks of him often. Bob's Dad took Bob along on many trips when Bob was young, and Bob is full of wonderful memories and stories about their travels and adventures. I'd encourage you to pick up Bob's book, *The Power of Who*. Next to *The Winsome Way* (written with a smile), it is one of the best books on encouragement of friendship and mentors there is.

Bob's wife, Cheryl, also gets credited often by Bob as his strength and joy alongside him. We need this in life. Mentors and allies. The importance of champions, mentors, allies, friends, and people who see the good in you and look to nurture it are the foundation of a great future for any individual.

For you, we begin your winsome journey by having already assessed earlier your own circle of winsome people. It's also important to look back from your earliest of life experiences to discover how people shaped your life.

Throughout the book and as part of each chapter, I'll share some key figures who built the qualities I today work to pass along to you via *The Winsome Way*.

Always Engage with Winsome People

FIND YOURSELF AND BECOME YOURSELF A WINSOME MENTOR, COACH AND ALLY

Mentor:

Noun

1. a wise and trusted counselor or teacher.
2. an influential senior sponsor or supporter.

Verb (used without object)

3. to act as a mentor:
   She spent years mentoring to junior employees.

Coach:

verb

1. to give instruction or advice to in the capacity of a coach;
   instruct: *She has coached the present tennis champion.*

Ally:

1. a person, group, or nation that is associated with another or others for some common cause or purpose:
   Canada and the United States were allies in World War II.

2. a person who associates or cooperates with another; supporter.

Winsome Coaching from Day One of Life

L.D. Snell and Kitty Snell

My Incredible, Extraordinary Winsome Parents

I was incredibly blessed by my parents L.D. (Lee) and Kitty Snell. I came along and was born late in their years. Mom 40 and Dad 43, they had already raised my two sisters, Janice and Judy, both talented and incredible daughters who were 14 and 16 years older than me. My dad used to say I was their "last gallant attempt at a son". Brought into this world by Dr L.J. Ekeler at Butler County Hospital in Nebraska on a freezing cold, sleeting Saturday at 7:12 p.m. My dad used to smile and remind me that I was "born during an episode of *Gunsmoke*". That was his favorite show, and it became a father and son tradition for over 20 years of watching the legendary Marshall Matt Dillon together. Marshall Dillon (James Arness) was winsome, for sure.

Needless to say, I was 'spoiled' in my sisters' eyes, yet as I recall and see in family photos, they were pretty fond of little 'Danny' and certainly added to any 'winsomeness' development in my life. Janice (Snell) McAllister and Judy (Snell) Page went on to win numerous school, community, and business awards. As I was just 'waking up' to the world in my first five years, I knew that I had parents and sisters who loved me, encouraged me, and sought to make 'Danny' the best he could be.

As I hope you might be able to do about your own respective hometown, I could write an entire book on the life lessons gleaned from growing up with my parents in David City, Nebraska. A town of 2,300, David City is a classic representation of the 'Small Town America'… a classic USA storybook place.

President Dwight D. Eisenhower shared his small-town thoughts:

> **For any American who had the great and priceless privilege of being raised in a smalltown, there always remains with him nostalgic memories of those days. And the older he grows, the more he senses what he owed to the simple honesty and neighborliness, the integrity that he saw all around him in those days.**
>
> *- Dwight D. Eisenhower*

Part of the gift of growing up in a small town is, indeed, the winsome culture that we are all in this together. The unity and spirit of the town lends to a mutual caring and interest in the special qualities and talents of each community member. People in the town often know who 'the best' in certain skills is. Who is the best mechanic, best golfer, best singer, cake maker, banker, or basketball player? Even the best knitter or quilter. Often, we look for that special quality and cheer it on. The togetherness of a small town lifts people to even greater heights. The 'incredible' in every person comes out and shines.

My parents were extraordinary in their efforts in David City to bring out the best in people, and in the community. L.D. and Kitty Snell held that special quality of wanting to lead people to discover what was possible in themselves and in our little community. What new and greater things might come to pass if only they would believe they can reach higher? That encouraging spirit stayed with me, and this book could not be written if it wasn't for my interest in YOU. You're reading this because you want to reach higher in life. I wrote it because I also want you to reach higher in life.

You've probably heard the phrase about someone you know, that they hold a 'Servant's Heart'. In the case of my parents, I was surrounded by two giant hearts for serving others' lives.

My Dad served as president or chairman of just about every organization in our small town. As a growing boy, I watched his heart and time be invested in organizations like the VFW / American Legion, American Heart Association, American Cancer Association, the local Chamber of Commerce, the Rotary Club, the Knights of Columbus, the golf club, the David City Foundation, the high school athletic booster club, and I could go on. If you've led an organization and know the commitment and the challenges and the joys of such efforts, multiply that by 30 for the years of service my Dad invested cheerfully, willingly, and 'winsomely'.

My father was a banker. He was always recognized as a community leader, yet never sought public office—or for that matter, he never sought public acclaim. He did it because he felt compelled as a businessman and a family man to make the community stronger. One of my fondest memories today —although it did not seem like it at the time — came about when it was those times for annual fundraising drives for organizations. In particular, I recall efforts for the American Heart Association, the American Cancer Society, the March of Dimes, and similar fundraisers of that time. With about 500 households in the community of David City, the best way to reach them in that era was direct mail. I still remember accompanying my dad downtown often to the bank board room. There, Dad and I would compile stacks with the national, state, and county information, and the 'ask letter' for donations. We prepped for our 'around the table production' as we prepared information to be placed in envelopes. Picture a 25-foot-long board room table. First, we'd lay down about 50 large envelopes around the table. Then, circling the table round and round, my Dad and I would lay on top of each one the envelopes a specific piece of information. Onto the top of those 50 envelopes went the brochure for the Heart Association, a story of success about how the AHA helped save a life, and the return envelope to send donations back. I remember him typing on a typewriter the personal 'ask' letter to the community. He always found a personal or community story of how he believed in the work of the organization seeking help.

We'd repeat this tabletop scenario until we had the 500+ envelopes completed. Then…my dad and mom would handwrite the names and addresses. No computer-generated peel-off address labels. No modern day 'print on demand' machines to run the names through. Just two dedicated, heart and soul winsome spirits who sought to serve. I look back now, thinking about circling that table as a powerful building block in my life. It became a 'stake in the ground' for me to serve others. I was honored to be asked to serve on the board of the Kansas City American Heart Association later in life. Let there be no doubt it was because of my parents.

My mother, Catherine Snell, was known as Kitty, an affection nickname my Dad gave her during the first year of their courtship in Gretna, Nebraska. Kitty Snell was, likewise, a special, winsome soul.

By today's standards, she could have made lots of money as a life coach. My mom was a "life coach" extraordinaire before the term life coach was even invented. Why? Because she came alongside so many people, particularly women of all ages, to teach them knitting, sewing, card games, crafting, and quilting. With the fervor of Russia's impact on American politics today, it might be of interest to know that Kitty Snell helped the women of David City produce a 50-foot-by-50-foot quilt that was accepted by the Kremlin as a gift to be showcased as an extension of world peace from the heartland of America. Way to go little David City town! My Mom encouraged women as mothers to stay active in community events and make a difference. Her spirit was truly winsome.

How did my parents pass it on? They poured into me the importance of being "involved in the place you call home", wherever that may be. With that as a foundation, at the age of 34, I ran and won a seat on the City Council of Shawnee, Kansas—a city of now 70,000 people in metro Kansas City. For ten years, I contributed my time, talent, and treasure, and from that, good things have come. Perhaps my strongest contribution was the development of "Shawnee Tomorrow", the leadership development program of the Shawnee Chamber Commerce, which has over 500 graduates, many of whom have gone on to serve in office or leadership roles in the community. My dad always said to, "Do your best and leave a legacy."

I encourage my children to always be a part of something bigger than themselves. And that's part of the message of this book. Be a part of something outside yourself that makes a difference in the place you call home.

As a side note… if we were able to reset any decisions, one would be to keep our boys in Boy Scouts. The character and discipline gleaned from the foundations of the Boy Scouts of America is priceless. If you are a parent reading this… get your children into Scouting. It is timeless and powerful life coaching at a young age, and they will remember it for a lifetime.

If you were not in such a family situation, the great thing to know as you're reading this book is that your life begins anew each and every day. The promise of opportunity is not a myth. Relationships, business, family, hobbies, and income can all be grown. YOU can be renewed and grown into something mighty! There can be a bright light of a future within you. By reading this book, you are boldly saying, "I will not go quietly into the night!" You will not let your candle of hope dim. You have a vision of the light, and 'winsomeness' is part of reaching it. The poet Dylan Thomas wrote his famous poem "Do Not Go Gentle into The Night" in 1951. The poem closes with the words, "Do not go gentle into that good night. Rage, rage against the dying of the light." He was writing the poem about his father, who was battling blindness, and he wanted his father to not give up and just let blindness ruin his life.

What's your 'blindness'? What is keeping you from seeing the bright light of your dreams? Think on this throughout this book. Keep that magic marker (or eBook highlight tool) hard at work. Revisit this book. Know that this moment, this hour, this day, this month, this year can be the season where your breakthrough to the light of the joy of feeling you're on your way begins.

I was fortunate to have parents and community that helped shape me in a winsome style. Small Town America at its best.

Earlier, you wrote down your Winsome People Inventory. I'll share mine with you later on, and it might help you revisit yours and add to your list.

CHAPTER 2
THE "W" FOR WILLING

Be willing. Having a willing attitude. Having a willingness to show up, be present, engage, look for good, and discover the extraordinary in people. Are you willing to do that? I believe you are. Absolutely when you picked up this book, you said to yourself, "I am (say YOUR NAME here), and I am WILLING to become and be WINSOME!"

You know people who are willing. They reach out to you. They are those people volunteering, helping at school, serving at church, coaching youth sports, raising money for a good cause, investing time to help others. If you have done any of these above in your past… stop here…stand up…and say to yourself or anyone in the room, "Hey, I am WILLING!" That's a great start! You've got the 'W' of Winsome on track in your life.

Now if you haven't, what a great moment. A time to review and assess that question which I believe you bought this book for: If I want to lead a more winsome life, then where can I become more willing?

A key to this whole book is recognizing that you do, indeed, want to grow and change and become something better. You have extraordinary talents! You know it. Close your eyes. Imagine what you would do if you would not fail? Yes, that is a timeless question, and it has been asked a thousand times. Many respond. Few are WILLING to begin and continue on the journey to being the extraordinary person God designed them to be. If you are not a person of faith, then you have worked hard by your own efforts to hone your skills and talents, and there may be something in you that's tugging, saying, "I'm close."

You know with just a few turns, decisions, commitments, goals set or renewed, you can reach up and become who and what you truly know you were meant to be. Be willing! Be willing today! Be willing tonight! Be willing!

Dictionary.com shares that the word "willing" means "inclined, cheerfully consenting, ready, given to, having a cheerful readiness." Moving forward, a few synonym words for the refreshed and willing you that will describe the new 'winsome' nature you walk around with are: eager, enthusiastic, happy, inclined, prepared, prone, amenable, pleased, favorable, cheerful, and enjoyable. Do you want to be considered any of these? I imagine you are, and that you are smiling right now. Good job! If you are, perhaps, in a minority who says, "These qualities are not me," then hooray, what a defining moment and opportunity for you! Who does not like a person with these qualities?

When you are truly willing—and not all people are—you say to the world, "I am willing to do that which the average, mediocre, or second place finisher type of person is not willing to do." You are the athlete who stays late to practice his shot or throw or hit extra balls or kick the soccer ball from different angles. You are the salesperson who gets to work before everyone to do the extra research on an account that sets him apart and wins the account. Or you are the mom or dad who sits just five minutes a day talking to their kids, which places them in a select, special group in America. Less than ten percent of parents speak daily for even five minutes to their children.

The willing person is the one Abraham Lincoln spoke of who live their life with the foundation in his quote:

> *"Most people are about as happy as they make up their minds to be."*
>
> *~ Abraham Lincoln*

You must be willing to stand out as a winsome person by choice. President Lincoln placed our nation onto a journey by ending slavery, because he was willing to see the positive benefits of our nation as a place where all men are created equal. He had that special ability to see our nation as more united and winsome.

Flash-forward to the modern day: we find a lot of leaders in industry who have built their reputation on winsome types of efforts. Marriott Hotels is where I exclusively stay by choice, and not by any benefit given here by this mention of their properties. The spirit of the Marriott Corporation permeates their chain, down to even the franchise owners and their employees.

Three Winsome Presidents

John Fitzgerald Kennedy
– Winsome Presence, Winsome Statesman

Growing up in David City, a small, predominantly Catholic community, having a Catholic President was a big deal. America had never had a Catholic President. It's a natural thing to be drawn to someone who holds a similar tie. We do it for schools, states, organizations, or most anything we've invested ourselves in. We want 'our team' or 'our guy/gal' to win. 'Winning' and feeling like you're on a victorious side of any endeavor is a big part of being winsome. Victories, both big and small, help bring about a more winsome walk. Back to Kennedy and his winsome way. The religious fears, even prejudices regarding the control by the Pope or the church of a Catholic President were unfounded, and in Kennedy's case, certainly not ever seen. I believe Kennedy's mystique stemmed from five areas. He had presence. He had a beautiful wife and family. He was quick-witted and engaging. He was a visionary statesman with a sense of history. Lastly, he was an image of youthful health. Our 35th President even became known simply as JFK. To anyone over the age of 50, these three simple initials bring to mind an instant image of his youthful, handsome, smiling face, and often the memory of a hero lost. To many generations, JFK reflected a winsome presidency. It was, perhaps, truly the first TV-based presence in America history. Now, let's break those five Kennedy winsome traits down and see if we can learn from them in our quest to be winsome.

PRESENCE:

Foremost, which is generally a key foundation of a winsome person, Kennedy held many qualities of a winsome presence, including: his good looks, warm smile, an engaging, charismatic personality, and a quick wit that warmed reporters and, thus, the nation. Presence is something everyone seeking a winsome way should contemplate. Everything from your posture, to your smile, to your eye contact are all important. Think on those things. Do you have your head up, smiling, looking to engage people as you enter a room? Or are you self-focused? Being winsome, having a 'winsome presence', especially in your role as a leader, means being ready to engage those around you in an upbeat and encouraging fashion.

SURROUNDING FAMILY:

JFK's beautiful wife Jacqueline (Jackie) reflected his youthful and charismatic manner. Most every woman in that day wanted to dress like Jackie and have the 'Jackie look'. Men and women were attracted to Kennedy's wife, as her beauty, even her accent, captured the American people. Kennedy's two children, Caroline and John, Jr. were the epitome of cuteness. Their childlike, joyous smiles and youthful charm – a trait of winsomeness – was also a part of the specialness of Kennedy. My late friend and mentor Zig Ziglar is often quoted talking about the 'home court advantage', meaning have a family or loved one that believes in you, supports you, and cheers for you. Kennedy, while certainly not perfect as husband, did truly seek to have Jackie and his children be a part of the history he was making.

ENGAGING QUICK WIT:

Oftentimes, people may say a person is 'quick-witted' or 'quick on their feet' and, then, say that they, themselves, are not. Well to that—and I use Kennedy as an example—I say quick wit and being engaging can be learned and can be taught. In Kennedy's case, growing up in a large family, the ability to fight for a spot of attention, or gain athletic prowess, or even the favor of his parents or in his surroundings came from being thrust into that arena to understand that to be the leader, to be the winner, you must compete. Compete not in a negative sense, but in the positive sense that you must strive to make yourself better, sharper, and grow daily. Credit the 'Kennedy clan'—as it is often referred to—as a shining example in our history of a family sticking together, working together, striving together to be better, to make America better. We have seen Kennedys lead throughout the years in public office and even more so behind the scenes in non-profit efforts. The Peace Corps, which was an incredible model for serving the world and maximizing a spirit of volunteerism, without first dumping taxpayer dollars wastefully, is just one of the many Kennedy legacies. Winsome? He engaged an audience of students when he announced it one day in Michigan. 10,000 people signed up to serve in a week. He cast a vision that stands today.

VISIONARY STATESMAN:

Well, we just spoke of the vision of the Peace Corps. That is one of Kennedy's visions. Kennedy—as with most winsome people—did not want to just be an average, common, or a status quo person. He wanted our nation, our people, our sense of history and effort to be a bold and visionary one. One of my favorite Kennedy visions and timeless quotes:

> *"We choose to go to the Moon! ...We choose to go to the Moon in this decade and do the other things, not because they are easy, but because they are hard; because that goal will serve to organize and measure the best of our energies and skills, because that challenge is one that we are willing to accept, one we are unwilling to postpone, and one we intend to win."*
>
> *~ President John F. Kennedy*

In your life, what are your 'choose to go to the moon' visions? Think on that. It will add to your winsome way.

YOUTHFUL HEALTHY IMAGE:

In 2015, a *Newsweek* article, citing various studies, shared that 71 percent of Americans are overweight or obese. Now, that should be a statistic and a 'vision' that a President seeks to cut in half by the year 2030. The 'go to the moon' vision we spoke of could have an earthly mission if we tackled the real foundation of our American health challenge. It would take a leader like Kennedy. Kennedy, when running against Nixon, seemed vibrant. His PT-109 military background, his energy and healthy glow, the Kennedy family football games on the front yard at Kennebunkport, all sent forth the image of a vibrant, high-energy leader. People want to follow the energy. For all seeking to follow the winsome way, an attitude and a daily effort to eat right, exercise regularly, and present ourselves as vibrantly as possible will truly make you healthier, wealthier, and wiser.

Ronald Reagan
– President and Inspiration

Presidential Winsome Personified

I arrived late to the meeting on the second floor conference room of the Lincoln, Nebraska manufacturing plant. The small, cramped room was filled with well over 100 people, all in attendance to learn about the Ronald Reagan for President campaign. I was there, as I had been inspired as I read the Reagan biography *Sincerely, Ronald Reagan* that had been written by his secretary during his gubernatorial years in California. It was filled with heartfelt stories of a man with a truly sincere heart for serving people.

Milan Bish, a prominent businessman in Nebraska at the time, was the Nebraska State Reagan Campaign Director and was in charge of the meeting. Also in the room was the then Governor, Charley Thone. Kay Orr, who would be both state treasurer and, later, Governor of Nebraska, were the two leading dignitaries in the room. At age 24, I was the youngest person in the room. Mr. Bish got up, introduced the dignitaries, and then proceeded to open the floor to anyone who wanted to share why they supported Governor Reagan for President. That was my moment.

I stood up, in my flannel shirt, and shared a story from the *Sincerely, Ronald Reagan* book about a military veteran, overseas, who would be away from his wife on their first wedding anniversary. The soldier wrote then Governor Reagan and asked if he would send a card from the governor's office, sharing the California soldier's love for his wife on their anniversary. The soldier wanted something special to happen for his new first anniversary bride, since he couldn't be there.

** As a side note, doing above and beyond is absolutely a winsome way in marriage, but I didn't know that at the time. As the Winsome Way series of books marches on, we'll be doing a book on the 'Winsome Marriage' and the 'Winsome Family'.

Back to Reagan. What did Governor Ronald Reagan do? He didn't send a letter or card. On this anniversary day, a Saturday, he apprised his staff, security, highway patrol, and local officials that he personally would deliver two dozen roses to this bride on their anniversary. The soldier had no idea until after the event took place. That struck me. As a romantic, sentimental guy, that made me think, *Now that's the kind of guy I'd like to be my President!* It was an above and beyond, serve the people, take the time to create a life-changing moment attitude. Reagan told no one but his staff. Only the neighbors awoken that Saturday morning by the flashing lights of the highway patrol, security, and the governor's limousine in their neighborhood knew. It was classic Reagan.

So, then what happened in that manufacturing plant conference room probably helped continue my desire to be involved in public service for life. You read the stories of my parents' local service, but this was big-time national presidential campaign stuff.

As the meeting was letting out, Milan Bish approached me and said, "Governor Thone enjoyed your story and would like to say hello to you." I had voted for Governor Thone, but had never met the man. The Governor asked me where I was from. When I said, "David City," the governor smiled and said, "You wouldn't happen to be L.D. Snell's son, would you?" To this day, as I write this, a love of my dad and pride for his heart and public service work swells up. "Yes, Governor, that's my Dad." I did not know that during some Nebraska banking conferences my dad had met Governor Thone and actually suggested a number of donors and advisers in the Nebraska banking community. My Dad had also, which I did not even know then, publicly endorsed candidate Thone at a major agricultural event during the Butler County Fair. Part of a winsome life is leaving a legacy. Can you imagine the legacy my Dad made me feel in that moment?

Milan Bish then said these words, "We loved what you shared tonight, and we'd like you to be the Lancaster County Campaign Chairman for the Ronald Reagan primary campaign." I smiled, froze, and then blurted out, "Gosh, I was my fraternity president, but I don't know the first thing about running a campaign." They laughed and shared that it was my youth they wanted to project. Reagan was the oldest candidate for President ever. People in their 20s were still a demographic that Reagan was not reaching. Lincoln is a college town. They simply asked of me to get up at gatherings, share the exact story I shared, and then introduce dignitaries who would speak on behalf of Reagan. So, there we have it. At age 24, I was told I would be the youngest county chairman of a county of over 100,000 people in America. I didn't realize he would go on to be one of the greatest presidents of our time, and that I would get to say I shook his hand and helped get him elected.

Now, humility is a key part of walking winsome, so I must share that my role was very small. Paid staff did the hard work, the true campaigning, the strategy, the get out the vote efforts. I was just a young face with energy and a love for the candidate.

I did get to meet Reagan twice. His only trip to Nebraska was to Grand Island and a quick in and out at the airport in a hanger close to Milan Bish's company. Prior to the big public event, there was a small gathering upstairs. We ate Wendy's burgers. I remember sitting two people away from Reagan. My biggest conversation and interest was speaking with then new Secret Service agent Tim McCarthy, who had been assigned to cover the candidate, and would, in 1981, be only the fourth Secret Service agent to ever take a bullet for a president. I remember how excited he was, and he hoped Reagan would win, because then, he'd get to be on White House detail. For the record, Reagan, McCarthy, and a young guy named Snell all three had 'single cheese, no onion' and a 'Frosty'. Even today, when I see a Wendy's, I think of that small room and eating close to Ronald Reagan.

As a winsome man, Reagan had some tremendous gifts. Like Kennedy, he'd enter a room with a vibrance and a smile. Reagan made famous his own personal touch of tilting his head. It is important as you develop your own winsome style that you find one or two things that set you apart. A gesture, a phrase, or something that people will remember you by. Reagan had a head tilt and his famous "well" that he used so powerfully.

Reagan obviously had training as an actor and speaker from his Hollywood days. That's an important trait of the winsome, too. Never stop learning. Always be a part of educating yourself. Listen to audio while driving, read a good book, stay up on what's going on in your community, state, and nation. People will follow a knowledgeable person. Let that be you!

William Jefferson Clinton

The Most Winsome President Alive

When Bill Clinton walks into a room, onto a stage, or even down the street, there is a glow. He is, very often referred to as, the most winsome man in politics today. One of the cornerstones of being winsome is being able to take heat, to fend off the negatives around you, and to outlast the negatives. That is William Jefferson Clinton. Clinton's personal presence, whether in person or with a crowd, is beyond compare. Ironically, Clinton's boyhood hero was President John F. Kennedy. Clinton's picture with Kennedy stands as one of the 42nd President's favorite. Clinton was at Boy's Nation in July of 1963. Who could know then that the picture with JFK would one day help elect Clinton to the White House? To be at Boy's Nation, Clinton had to be selected to Boy's State in his local Arkansas area. Then at Boy's State, Clinton won, and I'm confident he was 'winsome' in those high school years, the contest to represent all of Arkansas at Boy's Nation. What's the point? Like Bill Clinton or not, he was trying to be a leader, even in his high school years. If you are reading this and a high school or college student, take heart. What you do, who you reach out to, and your heart toward leadership and service may one day end up as part of your steppingstone to greatness. Winsome greatness. I do know that a winsome way does involve striving to do things that, often, a common man says they cannot do. Bill Clinton—and for that matter, his wife, Hillary Clinton—are such people. They do strive and attempt things that others might say can't be done. While I may not agree with their policy ideas in all accounts, I do applaud their decades of public service. The measure of a man or woman is often in their heart for serving others. Of the five presidents I've shaken hands with, a Bill Clinton hand was extended to me three times: twice in Washington, D.C. and once in Independence, Missouri. I remember one thing. Clinton looked right into my eyes, and into the eyes of every person he shook hands with. Eye contact is so essential to a winsome manner. If we study the Myers-Briggs Personality testing that has been highlighted about Clinton, he is considered an 'ESFP' or Extrovert, Sensory, Feeling, and Perception. Think on this. Absolutely Clinton was a people person extrovert. Without a doubt, his sensory skills to sense a situation, and move, speak, or act upon it was normally gripping to those around him. Feeling? Wow… who doesn't remember those famous and winsome words, "I feel your pain." Clinton does have an uncanny instinct for feeling the emotions and overall measure of a situation. His command of a room or setting because of this was powerful. Perception. He absolutely perceived America's heart, needs, and how to rally a crowd or nation. Clinton was a master at the ESFP personality traits, and we all can learn from his winsome techniques. In a later book of Winsome Public Service, we will focus more on the Clinton mystique.

The Serial CEO – Tom Henning

Not many people hold the title of CEO. Few hold the position in their twenties, unless they created their own company. Very few hold the title for over 30 years, as my winsome friend and college roommate Thomas E. Henning has. He became president / CEO of a bank in Hastings, Nebraska at the age of 26 and never looked back. He went on to be CEO of the National Bank of Commerce, then on to the financial services world as CEO of Assurity Insurance.

Winsome from the word go. I met Tom Henning during a Tau Kappa Epsilon (TKE) fraternity rush party. Tom and Larry 'Bernie' Austin were the key reasons I pledged the fraternity. Fraternal life often forces one into learning social skills that carry forth into life. Ronald Reagan – a winsome person – was a TKE. The founder of Starbucks, Howard Schultz, also a TKE – and a winsome person – has gone on to shape the world with his concept of the 'Starbucks Experience'. Starbucks creates a winsome atmosphere.

Right now, if you were a member of a fraternity/sorority, you might remember that special person, or perhaps it was a few people, who connected with you. They probably were a key reason for your membership. Odds are, if you reflect, they had a quality about them that made you see something special, upbeat, happy, and even energetic to be around.

Tom Henning's best winsome quality was his sincere interest in people. He made me feel like a fellow small-town Nebraska boy who he could relate to and who he wanted to help maximize my college experience. Henning was from Crete, Nebraska, and I, of course, from David City. Tom was outstanding at remembering names and places.

Tom selected me to be his 'pledge son', a role of mentor that is key in fraternal organizations. In that, I was thankful and honored. Thus, via Tom's campus high stature, I was fortunate to meet teachers, leaders, and key people around the university world, and was extended opportunities that Tom developed via his unique, winsome way. Oh yes, he also was especially gifted with girls, I fondly recall, and he married his college sweetheart, Candy, and they still are sweethearts still now, forty plus years later. They are a winsome couple.

CHAPTER 3
THE "I" FOR INTERESTED

When you reached to buy this book, something inside you leapt up and whispered, "I think this book might be the answer to help me grow." So right now, stop, stand up, applaud, and celebrate yourself. It's true! You want to grow! You want to shine! You want to be a difference-maker! Importantly for the I" of 'be interested' in all this, is being fully engaged and interested in a friend, your spouse, child, associate, neighbor, or even a first-time acquaintance you see something unique in. For many of you, it might be a young boy or girl you might be coaching in a youth sports program. Being interested is the greatest lifetime gift you can give them. As the title tagline shares, the winsome say is about discovering the extraordinary in those around you.

In the 2003 movie *Seabiscuit*, we re-live the true story of a horse who nobody believed in, who was small, had a quirky personality, and overall was not given a chance to be a winner in the horse racing field. One man, Charles Howard – the Interested one – watches from afar at first and, then, buys the horse. Then, he watches a loner-type horse trainer, Tom Smith, who had unusual observation, healing, and training techniques go to work. Howard hired him. Then, Smith, as a trainer took an "interest" in a too-tall, fiery, quirky – not unlike the horse, Seabiscuit – jockey whose temperamental personality seemed to mirror the horse he was to ride.

The movie was set during the downtrodden times of an era where depression had brought America to its knees. Our nation, not completely unlike the economic discouragement we just came out of, needed something to believe in. To see that a little guy, in this case, our horse, Seabiscuit, could rise up, even defeat a mighty champion, War Eagle, who in the movie, was billed as arrogant and above everyone else. You know the story. Tears throughout if you're like me. If you have never seen *Seabiscuit*, or haven't seen it in a while, that is your assignment for the coming weekend. Watch *Seabiscuit*.

What should you look for in *Seabiscuit*. Look for your opportunity to be uplifted. To believe again. To realize that if you take an interest in someone or some cause, like owner Charles Howard did, that your world, someone's world, even an entire nation might be uplifted. Discover that extraordinary quality in what's before you!

Pay attention now. If you wish to 'Walk Winsome' and live a winsome way of life, how INTERESTED you are in the person or cause in front of you will be a genuine measurement of your winsomeness.

Dale Carnegie, who happens to be buried in Cass County, Missouri, less than 20 minutes from my home, authored the book *How to Win Friends and Influence People*. One of his six principles is, "Be interested in people." As I mentioned early on, I have been influenced by many authors, speakers, pastors, coaches, and men and women who have impacted my life. Importantly, if you have not read Dale Carnegie's book, after you finish this book, go to our website and purchase *How to Win Friends and Influence People*. I'd like to have someone say one day, "Great minds think alike," after they read this book and his side by side. I only have about 15 million books to get into people's hands to match his readership. But you can help that happen! I believe in you!

Whoever is in your life, in the moment, or for a season, or for life, they are blessed by the creator with a gift, a talent, a special message or story worth sharing. No one should ever say that there is not an incredible and extraordinary specialness inside. You will discover the winsome way in yourself if you seek to develop that specialness. Each step counts. Every day counts. Discover today your own specialness and the specialness of those around you. Be INTERESTED in them.

> The dictionary describes INTERESTED as:
>
> **adjective**
>
> 1. having an *interest* in something; concerned:
> 2. having the attention or curiosity engaged:
> 3. characterized by a feeling of *interest*.
> 4. influenced by personal or selfish motives:
> 5. participating; having an *interest* or share; money involved.

There are some 'interesting' words within the definition. Concern. Attention. Feeling. Motive. Participation. When someone extends to us – with good and genuine motives - concern, attention, feelings, and participation in our lives, we feel good. We like that person, because that person seems 'interested' in us.

Jesus walked winsome. He took genuine interest not only in each person, but in humankind as a whole. The Apostle Paul writes to his Colossian friends and encourages them. In the Bible, in Colossian's 4, Paul writes and shares to (paraphrasing) 'devote yourself to being watchful and thankful. To be wise in how you act and speak in conversation. To make the most of opportunity. To be 'winsome' (some translations actually use the word winsome) in conversation, full of grace, seasoned with truth, and to make your message life-changing.' The message of goodness, cheerfulness, kindness, being appealing, and how to be happy is over 2,000 years old. Incredible that one of history's biggest persecutors and murderers of Christians would go on to be one of the most read and leading encouragers in history.

Every single person has a story. A business story. A life story. A family story. A hobby story. A health story. A faith story. A love story. The storylines could go on forever.

Bob Sherwood, one of those winsome wonders I share about later in this chapter, is the best interviewer I have ever seen. He has a childlike 'what is it?' and 'why?' type style of digging deeper into a person or situation. We can learn from this.

A piece of tremendous insight Bob Sherwood often shared, which flows perfectly as a winsome way to be, is that Bob believes each of us can 'birth' something special. He loves to discover someone 'pregnant' with an idea and then nurture them.

I personally know people who Bob, in his consulting role, has helped take a 'pebble' of an idea, and build a mountain. I remember Bob coached a high technology inventor, a mutual friend of ours, received a $7.2 million check, plus a five-year $400,000-dollar management role for an idea. Bob created the excitement, the value, and helped discover the extraordinary in the situation. Bob did so because he genuinely was INTERESTED in the young man's life, abilities, and future. Even today, a smile comes across Bob's face as he discusses that successful venture.

While being WINSOME is a way of life, the "I" of INTERESTED comes with the first realistic caveat of this book. You and I will not be able to take the level of being INTERESTED to a life-changing depth with everyone we meet. Often, you will have a feeling leap from deep inside you that tells you a special person is with you. That's when you explore and discover deeper what's extraordinary about this person, their life, idea, business, or story. So, part of true highest level winsome ability is that ability to discern and simply know when and with whom you are able to be that winsome life-changer.

Being INTERESTED starts in those powerful first 21 seconds of time together. I speak on Marriott Hotels later. The first 21 seconds you walk into a Marriott is what sets them apart. Through exceptional training, I can see in my imagination an 'antenna' on the heads of Marriott staff. The front desk is quick to greet. The morning breakfast person, the maintenance person walking the building, all bring 'winsomeness' to their greeting.

How and what do they do? Their heads are up, their smiles are on, their genuine 'how can I serve you' spirit is ready. It's the "Marriott Antenna" in their people that make them magnificent ambassadors in the travel industry.

Marriott hotel staff often create one of those WCM—a 'Winsome Celebration Moment'—during my travels. I use TripAdvisor as a way to honor, review, and 'celebrate' significant travel memorable moments for airlines, hotels, restaurants, coffee shops, and other spots. I highly recommend TripAdvisor. It's user-friendly and full of genuine reviews about places you might go to.

While hotels and other public places get paid to be on the upside of the winsome scale, each of us have memories of a person who took interest in our life. Next to my parents, who always tried to invest and grow my talents, I remember youth sports coaches perhaps the best, oftentimes when my confidence in that sport was not high.

Coaches who stand out with great memories of "BE INTERESTED" for my life are Jim Redler, my grade school basketball coach, my David City Aquinas basketball coach Dale Kerkman and his assistant coaches, Ross Ridenour and Father Bob Roh, and an American Legion baseball coach who later went on to coach at the NCAA major college football level, Pat Behrns.

All of these men saw the potential in my abilities and also saw clearly what I didn't have… confidence. The confidence that I could do it! "It" being play at a level equal to or above anyone on my team or community. I remember their big-time smiles of victory moments as a coach when I made a big play, the key basket, or looked like I was in command, mad, and was challenging the moment, giving my best. Do you know that feeling? When you rise above what you thought, or others thought you could do?

The NCAA basketball tournament ends each tourney night with the song "One Shining Moment", by David Barrett. It highlights memorable moments. Some are the agony of a loss or down moment, yet most proclaim a WCM (Winsome Celebration Moment). On a smaller scale, we should make sure we encourage our children and ourselves, as parents, to find a way to celebrate a teammate, friend or even fellow parent, when an athlete who is in our circle of community has his or her own shining moment.

Too often in our family life, marriages, business life, or community, we get busy, and don't invest the time and interest to 'celebrate' small day-to-day victories. We should never take for granted a simple reach to encourage, 'celebrate' with a kind word of enthusiasm for someone whose just had a bigger-than-usual moment. Imagine—or should I say 're-imagine'—life if we were all cheering each other on.

The Mission is ReMission – Pat Williams

Today, my winsome friend and sports executive Pat Williams epitomizes courage, energy, wisdom, trust in God, and love for people. All qualities of a winsome person.

Pat Williams is winning an ongoing battle with a rare form of cancer called multiple myeloma. He is a winner. Pat has written over 100 books, and I believe maybe by the time this book gets into circulation in a major way, my winsome friend, Pat, will have written his 110th book. Pat speaks across the nation, and I believe he is the best speaker many have never heard. When you hear Pat, you are changed. You remember Pat. He touches hearts and minds and spirits in his speeches. Like many great ones, Pat strolls through the audience to make his points.

Pat's encouragement and inspiration is a major part of the inspiration and spirit of this book, and to him, I owe much. His website is www.patwilliams.com, and his life story and sports and life success are profound and truly unprecedented.

In 1986, Pat traveled alone to Florida, basically to be part of the vision as an energetic sports professional and cheerleader, working 12 hours a day to convince investors and the city that a pro basketball team would come to pass. In 1987, the NBA announced that the Orlando Magic would join the league. Being the co-founder of an NBA team takes a winsome spirit. My friend, Pat Williams, is a true winsome leader.

Winsome and Smart - Robert J. Sherwood

Silicon Valley executive, entrepreneur of the year, business coach, expert courtroom witness, author, speaker, radio host, mentor, and friend. Bob Sherwood is able to hold many titles.

In 2006, I was asked to be the campaign director for Dr. Ken Canfield in his quest to be the governor of Kansas. Certainly, an honor and a thrill to be asked. Dr. Canfield and I had talked about my Ronald Reagan campaign leadership in Lincoln, Nebraska. We wanted a Reagan-like campaign. Positive leadership. Hope. Fresh ideas. Believe in Kansas! The Republicans wanted to pursue the sitting governor, Kathleen Sebelius, as if she was a 'bear in the woods.' I preferred a high road, positive leadership and messaging—not the negative politics of the last 20 years. I stressed that one such way was innovative leadership in the economy. Thus, Robert J. "Bob" Sherwood.

Bob Sherwood and I would be introduced to each other through many respected and knowledgeable economic leaders I knew as the 'go to guy' for an 'Economic Stimulus' program. Remember the 2008-09 federal efforts to stimulate the economy? The almost one-billion-dollar effort by Obama to jumpstart the economy? We were three years ahead for Kansas. We called it Kansas Tomorrow, and Sherwood was the author of it. We put forth Kansas Tomorrow prior to those national discussions of economic stimulus from Presidents Bush and Obama.

Dr. Canfield, himself a winsome fellow, should have become governor. He had a message that was inspiring, conservative, and foremost, unique, when compared to the other Republicans seeking the position to run against the incumbent Democrat and popular sitting Governor Kathleen Sebelius. Sherwood worked with us and did set forth our tremendous plan that even today would benefit Kansas or any state toward bringing in long-term revenue.

Robert J. Sherwood, Bob, as I would come to call him, is the smartest man I've ever met. His intelligence, coupled with a natural charisma and sense of liking new people and situations, truly places him as a winsome person to me. Bob hosted a national radio program called

Web Talk with Bob. Through my radio background, Bob asked me to be his co-host, yet I took on the persona of serving Bob as his sidekick, named Zip Daniels.

One exceptional winsome quality of Bob is both his 'insightful' and also 'inciteful' abilities. Bob has tremendous 'insight' to ask questions that truly bring out the extraordinary in a person, company, or, in our case, internet software or tool. Bob can also be 'inciteful', as he will ask challenging questions that incites emotion, fear, upset, or defensive behavior. I've only seen that 'inciteful' style come when someone deserves it. A winsome quality is to know when to challenge a person and not just do so without a foundation – in Bob's case, insight – that will allow the inciting to be fair and appropriate.

Bob grew up in Kansas City, Kansas. Quindaro Boulevard was his neighborhood. As with many urban communities, neighborhoods rise and fall. Coming from Quindaro, Bob exemplifies the extra effort, focus, determination, and commitment it took to rise to the great heights Bob achieved.

Bob has an extraordinarily unique mind. He thinks like both an engineer and a salesman. He can see and assist with integral designs, while always holding on the thought "How will we sell this?" Bob is an engineer by his BS and MS degrees from the University of Kansas, and Operations Research MBA from California State Hayward, then, a designer and crafter of both mechanical and electronic wonders. From humongous water pumps that lifted water over mountains in California to some of the first color monitor screens as a VP of RasterOps, Sherwood produced results. RasterOps, to anyone in the early days of computer screens, was the first color monitor to present true color. In 1986, it was considered as amazing as a new Apple product launch of today.

While Bob generally always has a smile when he greets new and existing friends, he also holds a unique quality of winsomeness, a very key quality that demands winsome credibility, integrity, and trustworthiness. I will touch on this later in the book. In brief, Bob holds a level of reasonable skepticism, and an analytical eye, that doesn't always jump forward saying "Yes!" Some people don't know how to take Bob's direct, straightforward message or questions. He speaks what they need to hear, and not always what they want to hear.

Bob's personal and professional background allows him to see challenges and then see solutions. That is his strength. No nonsense, positive, do-this-and-you-should-find-success solutions.

As with any winsome person, Bob has a personal presence, power, charisma, and style that draws people to want to be close to him and associate with him. I like spending time with Bob, and we meet about once a month. We share, 'brain-hurricane', laugh, challenge, and care. I enjoy this time. Later, in Chapter 10, I will talk about creating your 'Winsome Seven' and how time with them will be some of the best gift's you can share with one another.

Bob is a timeless, yet stylish, dresser. If you've heard me speak, you've seen me wear a pocket kerchief. Kerchiefs are timeless. In the 40s, 50s, and 60s, they were a staple for classic and powerfully dressed men. For about 40 years, they went away. When I met Bob Sherwood, he had a white kerchief in his suit pocket. It was a 'first impression' of class, elegance, power, and presence that left its mark. Today, part because I like its timeless message and part as a small tribute to my winsome friend Bob, I wear a pocket kerchief when I speak to large groups.

Attracting opportunity is a trademark of a winsome life. Along his life journey, Bob's depth and breadth of professional life took him to become the head of a venture capital firm, where he assessed and funded many startup companies. Bob had previously received a national 'Entrepreneur of the Year' award from Coopers and Lybrand so he was—and still is—a sought-after business consultant.

Bob is now in his 70s, but looks 50. He has athletic abilities in tennis and golf of a 40-year-old. He carries himself with the entrepreneurial flair of a 30-year-old.

I do not have a brother, although I am blessed with a circle of men who I can count on. Bob is one of those. He is the older brother type I always wanted, but didn't have.

What makes Robert J. "Bob" Sherwood winsome? It is a combination of many things that he developed in his life. That is a key throughout this book. Winsome people 'develop' themselves. Bob carries the best of a seasoned Wall Street, Silicon Valley, courtroom power and presence gentleman with gravitas, with the energy and enthusiasm of someone in his 20s discovering themselves. He never stops learning.

Social Chairman - CPA - Pastor Larry Austin, Jr.

To this day I consider "Bernie" my lifelong best friend. Like Tom Henning, I met "Bernie" – today called Larry - at a fraternity rush party. From that first seven seconds of introduction, he encompassed the winsome way that he truly holds even today for all who know him. Larry got his nickname 'Bernie' because of his uncanny resemblance to the *Room 222* TV show's character Bernie. Even his longer red locks bounced as he walked.

Larry was instrumental in my personal development in life as the older brother I did not have. He was there to listen, encourage, support, defend, and challenge me when he saw I needed a friend who would tell me what 'Danno' (as he called me) needed to hear, not just what I wanted to hear. That, my friend, is a real friend.

Larry's winsome style in college came, in part, with his affable, incredible style, and a special, creative manner of dressing. Over half of his days in college—yes, almost every other day—Larry wore bib overalls and no shirt. On the days when it was hot and when he wasn't in class, he would let down the bib overalls top, using the straps and buckles to create a belt to tie up his pants. Bernie's unique, winsome style of dress created somewhat of a fad at the TKE house, as many fraters began wearing the 'Bernie Look'. When you have a 'look' named after you… that is winsome!

Even in his fun-loving nature, Larry was a true leader. He began leading by serving as the 'social chairman' prior to his elected office. He was the best social chairman ever in TKE history. That's my story, and I'm stickin' to it. The fraternity parties and formal events were always the talk of the campus—and they were clean and not *Animal House*-like. A TKE party was always a sought-after event. His t-shirt designs still hang in my closet. Together, Bernie and I often served as the 'co-MC's' and entertainment, as we hosted many of the events. The bond with this friend grew as we planned many a memory-making moment in those college years. He was the house treasurer, as he would go on to become a CPA at Coopers and Lybrand. He then ascended to hold the office of Prytanis, the title for President of the TKE fraternity. A superior listener, Larry's sound, steady, solutions-oriented style with people creates a true respect and following that is to be admired. As he was about to be named a senior partner at Coopers and Lybrand and move into a six-figure income, Larry decided he wanted to go to seminary. And for that drive to Fuller Seminary in Los Angeles, I joined my winsome buddy. Yes, God can move mountains, as they say, and taking Larry and I from our collegiate escapades to men who know our talents and gifts and future belongs to the Lord God Almighty is a feat only a loving God could do. I say with a smile that out of respect for my great winsome friend, I have intentionally "forgotten" some of our college antics, as today he serves as a coach to pastors across the Midwest.

CHAPTER 4
THE "N" FOR NURTURING

As I write, you read, and we ponder this winsome way vision together, I know this. I have lived a life surrounded by some outstanding people who invested their hearts and minds to help me grow. They lived the "N" of WINSOME in that they were N for NURTURING. No matter how old you are, there is someone wiser, smarter, more experienced. My encouragement and challenge to you is to BE A NURTURER. There are areas I wish someone would have nurtured or coached me in, so I know that in that, I might take my knowledge and abilities and share them with another person who, as we are walking together, as we are WILLING and INTERESTED, we know we might NURTURE them to become more than they ever thought they could be.

These also should be part of your 'Winsome Seven', which we will talk about in Chapter 10.

Here's my soapbox and pontification on the subject of NURTURING:

If our society nurtured relationships as we could, the world would have more joy, wealth, peace, unity, faith, harmony, and stability. If a parent or neighbor or teacher or coach or an older, wiser, willing and interested person would nurture a fellow human, our world outcomes would be different. We'd have less crime, less divorce, less poverty, greed, war, prison population, single parents, and a whole host of societal challenges that damage our nation, as well as cost our economy billions of dollars. Here's my bold but truthful statement. I can show Washington, D.C. that a winsome and nurturing nation as to dealing with the 'breakdown of the American Family' could save over $500 billion dollars a year and cut the deficit in half in ten years. Congress will have to invite me to the Ways and Means committee to hear the solution, however. I will not be holding my breath. Sadly, the last of civility, let alone winsome spirit of most, not all, of our nation's leaders have placed us with a 'woesome walk' when it comes to trust and finding real solutions for our nation's challenges.

Former president Ronald Reagan, whom I shared my story of earlier, once said, "Government is not the solution to our problems; government *is* the problem." I studied this man. Reagan and Kennedy became the reason I sought public office. They both, in their winsomeness, were not government types. They were winsome leaders. Both hold legacies that inspired generations and causes.

Lest I digress to my old hobby, of which I got elected by surrounding myself with winsome people and a winsome campaign message, we should talk about your history, and your new winsome future as to you following a winsome way and your heart to become one who understands the power of those who NURTURE.

If you ever owned a dog, or, perhaps, a cat or other animal you truly wanted, you know that feeling of excitement in the first moments of ownership, the feeling of "How do I make the life of this special new friend as perfect and cared for as possible?" I remember as a child giving up my childhood stuffed dog, Blackie, so that the new puppy would have a furry companion to sleep with at night. We placed Blackie inside the giant cardboard box we got from the local David City Hinky Dinky grocery store. We placed a blanket, Blackie, and underneath the blanket, an old wind-up alarm clock that made the ticking sound to emulate the heartbeat of the puppy's mother. Do you remember your first pet? Did you nurture it's first days as I did?

Now, let's fast forward in life to those who may be parents. Wow... now do you remember that first moment of holding that baby in your arms? With vivid clarity, I remember holding the tiny, and the most beautiful baby ever at that time, Sarah Elizabeth Snell, on August 21st, 1990. She almost fit in my hand, and for sure, my one arm, as she rested on my forearm. It was a priceless memory-maker moment. For sure a WCM. If you are a Mother, do you recall the moment that little life was laid on your chest? The life you had nurtured while inside you by getting checkups, eating well, keeping fit, taking special supplements and otherwise, in anticipation of that day now here. As a husband and father, I remembered caring for my wife in special nurturing form to assure that they, and our baby to be born, were especially safe and cared for. I recall with each of the children speaking to my wife's stomach, even singing to the children in the womb. That feeling of nurturing before the birth then even becomes larger and more intense once you actually see the little life before you. Special bedroom, bathroom, and clothing needs were usually set already. Little toys ready to be watched as they hung above the baby's bed.

If you're a parent, take a moment to recall the specialness of those days. Part of being winsome is to have more of our 'Winsome Celebration Moments' (WCM). Reflect on your children's first days. In fact, if they are near you or your able to call them, reach out right now and tell them how special their first moments, hours, and days were. Watch what they say. Children need to be nurtured to fully know the first moments of their birth. By doing this, you are teaching them to live a more winsome life. It's important as you 'walk winsome' to take the time, make the time, to create moments that cause a pause. An old saying often used by legendary golf professional Walter Hagen, himself a winsome fellow, for sure, is, "Stop and smell the roses." Hagen did not originate the saying, yet he probably made it famous more than anyone. So, hats off to Walter Hagen.

I owned a putter as a teenager with Hagen's autograph stamped on it. Little did I know that some 40 years later, I would be reflecting back upon that putter as part of this book. That's part of the winsome life you can have, too! Reflect back on people, toys, events, coaches, teachers, and yes, golf clubs, to see if they are 'stamped' upon your mind as part of your winsome growth. You'd be amazed at how our growing up, like my experiences with the milkman, Bill Eller, and bus driver, 'Mr. Doughnut', will circle back into your memory as shaping your winsome walk.

> **Dictionary.com describes the word 'nurture' as:**
>
> verb (used with object), nurtured, nurturing.
>
> 1. to feed and protect:
>
>   to nurture one's offspring.
>
> 2. to support and encourage, as during the period of training or development; foster:
>
>   to nurture promising musicians.
>
> 3. to bring up; train; educate.
>
> noun
>
> 4. rearing, upbringing, training, education, or the like.
>
> 5. development: the nurture of young artists.
>
> 6. something that nourishes; nourishment; food.

The origins of the word stems back to the 1300s and primarily speak to the concept of 'feeding the offspring'.

Well, there you have it. Your new winsome walk has included you being willing to keep your eyes and ears open to a person or cause worthy of extra heart and effort, then being interested in someone genuinely, and taking that next step to 'NURTURE' the person or cause.

Oftentimes—especially in the formative years of a child that can even stretch into the twenties—there is an opportunity to make a life-changing impression upon a life. Your willingness, interest, and nurturing can take someone headed in the wrong direction and place them on the road to success or, at least, for sure a path greater than they could imagine. Stories abound of lives changed by a mentor, coach, or older man or woman who cared enough to impact a life.

The Bible speaks of nurturing often.

One of the most famously quoted verses is Proverbs 22:6, as it shares the importance of nurturing character and faith.

> *"Train up a child in the way he should go; even when he is old, he will not depart from it."*

Dr. Dan Erickson – His Ever-Nurturing Trademark – *"You're the Best!"*

Dr. Dan Erickson now in Heaven, was 110% winsome. All the way. I remember the winsome moment he walked up to me at church in 2006. He said, "How ya doin'? My name is Dan, and for some reason, I think I'm supposed to get to know you." Being a Dan myself, loving his big smile and knowing this guy was an awesome speaker and motivator around the country certainly gave me a memory-making moment.

Each of us encounters a person we admire, follow, trust, and seek the counsel of. If you're reading this, to be truly winsome, you must find mentors and people you emulate. Dan Erickson was such a man.

Dan Erickson was the reason I helped co-found an organization serving blended families. Dan was also the reason I spoke at men's conferences across the country. He challenged and, foremost, nurtured my talents to serve others. He always had a positive word or quote. Ever the encourager and 'nurturer'.

Dan wrote a book called *Finding Your Greater Yes*. It was an inspirational, faith-based message about discovering your potential and using the gifts and talents inside you. Dan felt—and I agree—that usually something inside you whispers in your life, "I could do that," or, "I really think that is what I'm supposed to be doing." Then, of course, he outlined the 'how to' go about it.

Every time I spoke with Dan, he held a calm, steady message of hope, inspiration, and encouragement about using my personal potential and gifts. When someone does that to you, listen. In most cases, it is something of the winsome spirit that is in them that drives their comments. Dr. Dan, as he was affectionately known, pushed me to write this book and nurtured the confidence to share the message.

Dan usually sets up his office at a local Starbucks or Panera Bread. Men who had been touched by Dan's heart and words, and sometimes women, would stop by because they know they'll find a Dr. Dan smile, encouraging word, a special challenge to rise up better and higher than they think they can. Dan was a man of God. Now each of you may not want or seek a spiritual nurturer, and that is up to you as an individual. Yet if you are a person of faith, you may remember the Dr. Dan in your life.

The Kindergarten Bus Driver - Bob 'Mr. Donut' Donner

The yellow bus is an American tradition and an American tradition in which I'm sure 95 percent of you reading this book have ridden at least once in your lifetime. My big first day of kindergarten was upon us. I was nervous. Bob 'Mr. Donut' Donner would prove to be a lifelong winsome memory. The David City Elementary School bus slowly pulled around 5th and K Street that September morning as I was sitting on the front porch, blessed to have my mom there sitting with me. Even my dad, who waited before going to work, was there with Super 8 movie camera in hand, ready to capture the moment. Now on this particular day, I cannot tell you, without a smile and red face, the story of my first sight of Mr. Donner, the kindergarten bus driver. Why? Well… because as I stepped off the porch anxiously toward the street about 150 feet away, I turned back – and remember, this is captured on Super 8mm film – and the look on my face turned scared and embarrassed. I had pooped my pants. Yes, the whole embarrassing truth, it is revealed. I pooped my pants in fear my first day of kindergarten.

I raced back to the steps that day and told my Mom. My dad went out to quietly – so as not to cause me peer embarrassment – tell Mr. Donner that I had a small accident and that he would drive me today to school. Quickly, I changed pants, and we rushed to David City Elementary. I even beat the bus, as it had to make the other pickup stops along the way. So, I was there, clean and ready to go for Day One.

I remember striding in with Dave Kozisek and Doug Pillen, who became my kindergarten buddies. They told me "You missed it! The bus driver, Mr. Donner, gave us donuts! We're gonna call him Mr. Donut!" Bob Donner was probably already 70 years old and very slender and frail, yet held a powerful and welcoming countenance. A 'winsome' countenance. Joyful eyes. He loved his job, and he loved people. He was one of those people who everyone loved and remembered.

Now, I speak to hundreds of thousands of people, on stage and through media, yet on my first day of kindergarten, my first day on stage in school life, I pooped my pants, as I was so nervous. There you go! We can overcome fears! Right.

Bob Donner helped show me the impact of a first impression, which is powerful in any relationship. Mr. Donut always had a giant and enthusiastic greeting when he opened the bus door. He would encourage, if not demand a 'big smile' as the price for his bus ride to kindergarten. When we left the bus, everyone would turn back and wave and shout, "Bye, Mister Donut, see you later!" He'd return at 12:30 to take us back home. Mr. Bob Donner, hereafter referred to as Mister Donut, knew how to capture the hearts of his young riders. He promised donuts every Monday if we would behave Tuesday through Friday. He 'nurtured' our young lives into respectful ridership. The power of persuasion? A trade of goodness for gooey donuts? A simple, "Let's all make the bus ride a fun thing." I never got to thank him for his heart…and the donuts. Bob "Mister Donut" Donner died in the early 80s, but his winsome way of nurturing young lives echoes on, in this book and beyond by the lives he touched. Ask yourself this question, "Can I find a little 'Mr. Donner' in me?"

Three Winsome Women

I imagine most people would laugh if I said I was a shy boy of sorts growing up, especially when it came to women. Three women who I remember made significant contributions through simple, powerful words that I want to quickly highlight. All three fall into that category of someone speaking life, confidence, vision, and power into a person's spirit. I once heard a pastor say,

> *"You can change a life with a word, a look, or a touch."*

That is a powerful quote for this **winsome** book, because those three words are worth breaking down and thinking of those three impactful ways to reach someone… a word, a touch, or a look.

From the first days of life when we started to walk or accomplish simple childhood milestones, our parents say, "You can do it!" and "Yes, there you go…come on… almost there," along with other words of belief in you. Somewhere along the path of life, the naysayers—we'll refer to them as 'woesome'—grab us. Later on, we talk about the 'woesome' and why to be 'mindful' of them. The WINSOME person, which you aspire to be, is one who speaks powerful words of 'can do'.

The Nun

Sister Dorothy was a dynamic, upbeat, and cheerful nun at Aquinas High School in David City. She taught English. My sophomore year, she became one of my favorite teachers. Why? Because after about the second month, she told me, "Danny, you are one of the best writers in school. You're creative, use good adjectives, and tell good stories to draw readers in." She then said those magic words: "Who knows, maybe one day you'll write a book?" The power of a word spoken into the life of a young person I say again is key. The Bible speaks to the power of the tongue in Proverbs 18:21 where it shares; "death and life are in the power of the tongue…"

When you are 16 years old and having had traditional nuns be sterner and follow the rules or get whacked (my Catholic readers will smile here), Sister Dorothy was a WOW! She led the "be a nurturer" way to her winsome walk with God and her students. Even as I have written this and you read this, I say, "Thank you, Sister Dorothy… I'm writing that book that you spoke into my heart some 45+ years ago." I am very thankful for my parochial education, the nuns, the priests, the teachers, the coaches, and guidance I received there in little David City at St. Mary's Grade School and Aquinas High. In a season of TV when *The Flying Nun* was the most famous of nuns, Sister Dorothy was, indeed, the 'Winsome Nun'.

The Cook

Onward to the University of Nebraska and my TKE fraternity days. Ronald Reagan, as I shared earlier of my story of with him, was a member of TKE, along with Starbucks founder Howard Schultz and NFL QB great and now Fox sportscaster Terry Bradshaw, and many more. Our TKE house cook, Hattie Payne, was an incredible nurturer, and she blessed young men's lives for years.

Hattie Payne was a stately, elderly black woman, full of grace and God's love, yet definitely full of fire when she needed to be. I remember her most by the 'look' she would give a fraternity brother. Her deep, soulful, dark eyes extended love and firmness. She often would stop, pause, and gaze into a young man's eyes when someone was trying to grab more than their share of food, iced tea, ice cream, cake, or especially the 'scooter pies', and lock on their eyes. She could look deep into your soul. She would often challenge us with a, "If your Momma was here…" Something about getting the "Hattie Look" was significant. She was working to nurture and bring out the good and honorable ways in all of us. Hattie would then often use the words with that 'look' that stay with me, and many TKE fraters, throughout life, "Young man! I believe *you* are better than that!" You could hear it echoed throughout the house for years, as that message would be repeated by fraters when one man spotted another being less than honorable. How could anyone try to sneak an extra scooter pie if you were being encouraged with a soulful "I believe in your goodness' look from Hattie. And how can I go through life without feeling Hattie's 'look'? Hattie was about 60 years young, although we thought her around 40ish. I'd love to sit with Hattie today and listen to her years of stories about fraternity cooking and hear her wisdom, so she might nurture me again.

The Queen

You will read soon and hear often about two of my part-time college jobs as I matriculated through the University of Nebraska. Pat Vifquain was the 'station manager' for the Avis Rent-a-Car location at the Lincoln (LNK) Nebraska Airport. I always thought it should be named for somebody, but that's for another day and motivation when I return to Lincoln to speak and inspire.

Pat had run the Avis station for a long time. She was the most tenured airport person around. Everyone knew Pat. Pat had most ideas, plans, and events run by her first for her wisdom and blessing. She was the Queen of the Airport, loved and respected.

I applied for a job at Avis. I remember Pat's handshake, warm eyes, and welcoming smile. I foremost remember that she gently touched my sports jacket and immediately placed a 'We Try Harder' sticker on my right lapel. She stepped back, looked at it, and said, "That looks good, Dan. You look like you have the right amount of 'We Try Harder' spirit, and have a good smile, so let's go talk." I have always remembered Pat placing that Avis sticker on me and just knowing and feeling in that very moment that I was "Dan the Avis Man". Before we even conducted the interview, the 'touch' of placing the image of Avis upon my lapel sold me that I wanted to be a part of the team. In her 20 years of managing this location, Pat told me she had 'never hired a man'. Why? I am smiling big here. I don't want to get caught in the middle of that, but let's just say that Pat always looked for, and was successful, at hiring the most beautiful girls to man the counter. Many a traveler, who didn't already have a car rented, marched directly to the Avis counter. We got 80 percent of the non-reservation customers, over Hertz and National, because Pat hired 'winsome smiles' to win the moment.

Pat hired me. I worked 90 days cleaning and vacuuming cars first before graduating to the counter. I spent almost two years as 'Dan the Avis Man'. Pat Vifquain was a nurturer. Without her seeing the good in Dan Snell, as seeing the good is a winsome trait, I would not have experienced some great life moments. I got the thrill and sports spectacular moment as I experienced honor of shaking hands with Paul "Bear" Bryant, legendary Alabama football coach.

Without my Avis job, I would not have met this sports legend. It was a fall Friday afternoon in 1977 when the Crimson Tide flew into Lincoln airport as they prepared to take on Nebraska. By the way, with a smile, I can share for trivia buffs that the Huskers upset the favored Crimson Tide that Sept 17th Saturday afternoon by a score of 31-24. To the story. As our Avis booth was directly at the bottom of the escalator that would bring the Alabama team through the doors to their buses, it posed an opportunity to have some fun. Avis, who gave us red blazers to wear, somewhat matching Alabama red, offered me a creative opportunity. In the "E for Enroller" chapter you will read about my high school golfing story friend Gary Novotny. He worked at a clothing store at the Gateway Mall and let me know he was saving a houndstooth hat for me to buy. I had shared with my friend my idea of trying to meet Bear Bryant, and it worked. As the team and entourage, including Alabama State Patrol guarding "the Bear" was coming down the escalator, there I was in my Avis red blazer and respectfully wearing a 'look-alike' houndstooth hat. The escalator met the bottom floor, the doors not more than 20 feet ahead and out to a bus. I thought, "Wait, darn it, with all the crowd and news media shouting at him, he didn't see me." And I had paid $38 for that hat! But then—and a smile comes even now, as I share again what happened next—right before he exited the airport doors, Bear Bryant stopped, turned, and strode about 15 steps to the right of those doors and reached out to me, shook my hand, and said simply, with no smile even on his face, "Nice hat, son," and then turned and walked away and out the door. I had shaken the hand of an American icon and had a forever sports memory.

My biggest thrill as 'The Avis Man' came on June 20th, 1977. Elvis Presley was performing what would become one of his last concerts ever. He would die of an overdose within 60 days. For his entourage, they contracted with Avis for 15 rentals cars and three vans. They were to be taken across the tarmac to the private hangers. Elvis was flying in on his private plane, 'The Lisa Marie', named after his daughter. We also shuttled in a special limousine from Omaha. It would be my job that day to drive the limo over onto the private Lincoln airport terminal tarmac, 100 yards from where 'The King of Rock and Roll' would step from 'The Lisa Marie'. With excitement, I entered through the private gates and drove slowly toward where I was directed. I stopped where they waved me to. Immediately after parking and getting out of the limo, one of the Elvis entourage approached the limo from the plane, and quickly worked to dutifully scoot me away. Graciously, I began to walk away, but turned back and waved to the King. He waved back and smiled. I had been 100 yards from Elvis at the age of 21. June 20th, 1977, the King of Rock and Roll smiled at me. Certainly, in his own special entertainment giant way, Elvis was winsome legend.

I am thankful that Pat Vifquain's 'nurturing touch' of placing that 'We Try Harder' sticker gave me my Bear Bryant and Elvis moments. I was offered a job after college with Avis, so perhaps her hire was a good one. While I did not continue on at Avis, I still 'touch' Avis employees wherever I fly with an Avis story or two and talk about Pat and my 'Dan the Avis Man' kinship to them. Pat Vifquain was a 'Nurturer'.

CHAPTER 5
THE "S" FOR 'SOLUTIONEERING'

In our journey toward walking winsome, or 'The Winsome Way', we've covered the importance of being 'Willing', being 'Interested' and being 'Nurturing'. All three take a decision to BE and told to LIVE out those qualities as we embrace those around us.

Now, we venture further and deeper into being a difference-maker after we've discovered, and believe, in the extraordinary of the person we're going to unleash our winsomeness unto. Now there's a term: "Unleash the Winsomeness." You are more powerful than you thought! You're unleashing in your own life as you read and fully catch, and believe, the vision of the winsome person inside you.

> **Dictionary.com says of the word 'solution':**
> - the act of solving a problem, question, etc.
> - the state of being solved
> - method of solving; an explanation
> - the process of determining the answer to a problem
> - the answer, itself

The 'S' of Winsome means "BE A SOLUTIONEER." Solutioneering is the action verb side of solution. That's what everything winsome often needs. Action! To be winsome, to walk winsome, to live winsome, to encourage winsome…takes action!

I have always strived to live the concept of not just pointing out problems or challenges, but to find solutions. Throughout our 19 years of marriage, I have always encouraged our six children to look for the opportunity in the challenge, to be the person who is offering the solution, not focusing or pointing to the problem.

I am happy to say that all of our children, now ages 22 to 29, each have had shining moments and success in their life. They have "Attitude is Everything" plaques in their homes, dorm rooms, or apartments from a traditional Christmas gift I share often. If I see one great plaque, I buy many of them. One for each of the children and one for our home.

In the above gifting story lies yet another way you can be a 'solutioneer' in the life of someone you care about. Or even as you build your strong base of winsomeness. Find a saying, or a few sayings, that resonates with you. Fill your 'space'—your home, office, or surroundings—with that messaging. You'll be amazed what it does for you and what it does for those who see your heart through these messages. Hobby Lobby, a winsome company, has some of the largest inventory of plaques, paintings, wall murals, and other inexpensive opportunities to fill your life with winsome words.

I first came across the phrase 'solutioneering' by accident, when I was looking for the book *Visioneering*, by Pastor Andy Stanley, of Atlanta, and I googled the wrong term, as I thought 'Solutioneering' was his title. By the way, his book, *Visioneering*, is a must-read. I got two great concepts out of the moment. Visioneering AND my term used here: 'solutioneering'.

Solutioneering was developed by R. Buckminster Fuller, who described himself as a "Comprehensive Anticipatory Design Scientist". Okay. I get that, and you may, too, if you say it three times slowly like I had to do. Remember engineering and other studies Mr. Fuller may have excelled in were not part of my matriculation through the University of Nebraska. Probably because such esteemed and higher intelligence level courses could have threatened my prestigious 2.2 GPA.

I've read and believe Mr. Fuller's goals were more solutions to large-sized world, earth, and non-human things, more than the basis of our purposes in the winsome way. In fact, I now give Mr. Fuller his last hoorah here, due to the purpose in our winsome walk together, that we are dealing with greater and more powerful goals… to develop a person into their highest and greatest potential! To develop you and see you develop others! Now that's winsome!

Without a doubt, one of the greatest visionaries of our modern time is Steve Jobs of Apple. His creativity, his intensity, his steadfast drive to place real solutions to life's challenges into the hands of people has made history. I can recall the Apple II, the first personal computer that came in a plastic case, and had color on the screen. From there, I owned an Apple SE, and have since purchased iPods, iPhones, iPads, Mac Book Pros, and other Apple products for myself and my family. We have seen his 'solutioneering' and embraced it.

Steve Jobs put it more simply and better than anyone has in years as to his goal of 'putting a computer in the hands of everyday people'. That vision, and the real solution that truly caught people into his solutioneering mindset. It's predicted that by 2016, over 2 billion smartphones will be used worldwide. 2 billion 'computers' in people's hands. 2 billion. That's solutioneering that has changed our planet.

Steve Jobs was a solutioneer. He watched society. He saw day-to-day challenges and turned them into opportunities.

Another great American, President John F. Kennedy, wanted our nation to be seen as the leader in the world of technology and space, so that we might feel truly like the winners we were after World Wars I and II President Kennedy's bold solution was that, "This nation should commit itself, before this decade is out, of landing a man on the moon and returning him safely to earth."

Think about that. He had a solution. Set a date. Engaged the greatest minds of NASA and beyond. We did it. That is 'Solutioneering' at its best.

Kennedy set our goal. Set forth the vision. Created the excitement. Built the best team NASA had ever seen. And on that July evening of 1969, within the 'end of the decade', Kennedy had proclaimed, I sat with my father in front of a 19-inch black-and-white TV to see Neil Armstrong make history.

Neil Armstrong made the 'one small step' phrase eternally famous.

> *"That's one small step for a man, one giant leap for mankind."*
> - June 20, 1969 10:56 p.m. CST

Let's now, this day, this week, and this season, as we 'land' on our own winsome moon declare boldly as we touch down. Let's help you take one small step this day reading this book. One giant leap for you and your family. Let's plant a stake in the ground toward reshaping our outlooks, just as Armstrong planted the American flag on the moon.

Now that is exactly what I want to do for YOU!

For this, I'm asking of you to not just nod, agree, smile, or think, *Yes! I want to set forth my JFK moon mission.* So, stop, if somewhere in your house, apartment, dorm room, or closet you have a white board, a flipchart, maybe some large construction paper, or even better, a window you can write with erasable marker ink on. Yes! Stop. Get up. As JFK did, walk to your own 'microphone' (your writing place) and declare your mission. Even better, if you have a video camera, or even your phone, create your mission statement. Date it. Email to yourself, and please email it to me at video@thewinsomeway.com. I want to see it. We might use it during one of our webinars or coaching sessions. We'll encourage you and celebrate you with extra gusto if you email your video.

Be sure to set a date when you will boldly and daily walk winsome toward. Let's commit ourselves, you to do this and me to help, to 'landing' you on the winsome side of the world!

Together, we are solutioneering. We are saying, "Hey, I want to be different, more positive, more upbeat, more cheerful, more optimistic, and, foremost, I want to celebrate more!" Celebrate your small things in life, and that will lead to the big things, whatever your goal or purpose.

BEING A SOLUTIONEER FOR OTHERS.

Most every day of our life, if we're active and engaged in business, family, or people, we come across someone who's in need of an idea, encouragement, or a solution. Now is our chance to give something back. Now, you can become an outward solutioneer.

In his book, *The Tipping Point*, Malcolm Gladwell speaks of people who are "connectors" and "mavens". Gladwell notes "connectors" often know a significant number of people that are often trendsetters, and "mavens" are people who are on top of the latest and most valuable information. Mavens are well-read and have the inside scoop in many situations. Mavens and connectors are different in that, sometimes, mavens are less social and less adept in interpersonal relationships, like connectors. Whatever you lean toward, either one of these noted talents make for a 'solutioneer' when their heart is interested (remember the "I" of WINSOME) in helping a friend or acquaintance discover how to rise up. When we are part of something rising up, or feel the momentum of a person, situation, team, or organization, you know you're part of something special. Momentum, by definition, speaks to the 'impetus gained' by an object or subject.

Rising up leads to a winsome walk. Rising up, whether for ourselves or helping another is a key to the winsome heart of a solutioneer. When we lift another up, we send forth a ripple into the world for eternity. One never knows the echo effect of helping someone discover their solution.

When you discover the joy and personal satisfaction, even exhilaration, of helping another person find their solution, their passion, their purpose, then you're truly reaching the winsome way.

You Always Remember Your First Sale – BOB BALDERSTON

"Hi Folks! I'm Bob, from Blue Springs Ford!" That incredible and iconic self-made brand of energy, enthusiasm, and salesmanship resounded on radio, TV, billboards, and print ads for well over three decades in the Kansas City area. Bob Balderston, owner of Blue Springs Ford and one of KC's most dynamic Ford dealers is special to me. Bob is an exceptionally winsome fellow. He was my 'first sale' of my professional sales career. He was the very first business owner I ever sold software to during my career at ADP Dealer Services. I'll never forget the effervescence that Bob lived with and infused into all around him. Bob is a true WCM – Winsome Celebration Moment – type of guy as he represents the very first sale I ever made in my professional sales career.

I smile as I remember Bob turning down, in a very winsome manner, our first price proposal with a timeless comeback in an effort to negotiate. "Dan, I want you and ADP to make money. I want everybody to make money. Just not all at once… off of me." He 'encouraged' me – again encouragement in the midst of my very first sales process and deal—to "Go back to your Regional VP, and tell him Bob needs to pay less of the data center electricity than ADP wants in this deal." It worked. I went back. In my most winsome way (gleaned from all the winsome mentors of my life), I talked our VP into another seven percent off, and I had my first sale of my professional career.

I'll never forget Bob Balderston smiling, signing the contract, and encouraging me that I will do well in this profession. I guess he was right. Thank you, Bob! You genuinely bring a smile every time I think of you.

The POSITIVITY GUY – MICHAEL C. SAUBERT, SR.

If you woke up every morning with the national news blaring, I mean business headlines and media shouting, that the place you call home was trying to reorganize and recapture it's once glorious past struggles to stay positive? Well let me tell you about a guy who does and is a national leader in positivity. He is a bright light in an arena of darkness.

Mike Saubert, Sr. is a classic American story. Of love of God, country, family, company, and people. Mike is Mr. Positivity and holds a heart to lifts up others wherever he goes. Whether in the workplace, at church, as a volunteer for many veterans or community organizations or his family. Mike's wife Kimberly, daughter Danielle (dietitian and YouTube sensation) and sons, Eric (an NFL tight end), Mike Jr. (acclaimed actor) and Timothy (college) and even his four dogs all know that the smile and energy of Dad is positive. These days, especially in his workplace he brightens the world.

Mike Saubert works for Sears. Sears, an American iconic retail giant and tradition. Yes, Sears, where much of America has walked through their doors for decades. We owned Craftsman tools, Kenmore appliances, and DieHard batteries. Many don't know that Sears started Allstate Insurance. The history and business success of Sears is truly unprecedented as to its milestones and successes, yet we come to the last few years, and due to the changing economy, has closed stores nationwide and has scrambled to take on the online giant Amazon and other companies. Sears has struggled and, thus, the headlines and the challenges.

Mike is the director of design for the Kenmore division of Sears. He been a part of Sears designing household items that millions have in front of them today. Imagine as your read this that a toaster, coffee maker, stove, refrigerator, dishwasher, or washing machine being used all across the nation has your signature to sign off on it. Kind of a very empowering feeling, huh? Mike remains optimistic and positive always. And he has guardian angels.

Mike holds an incredible series of life events that could easily discourage most anyone, including a potential near-death experience during his time serving in the U.S. Army as a Blackhawk helicopter pilot. Mike was moments away from takeoff with a crew of eight soldiers onboard when a master caution light said something's not right. So instead of launching, Mike had to taxi to the maintenance unit. As they were waiting for the maintenance unit, three Iraqi missiles landed in the exact spot they were headed to take off. Had they not had that engine component failure light, Mike Saubert, and seven other great Americans, would not be here today.

JAMES MALINCHAK – *Secret Millionaire and Solutioneer*

I remember some of the first words James Malinchak uttered to me the moment we met was, "Dan! I followed what you've been doing with blended families, and I want you to know I so believe in you! You're going to do great work, and this conference will help you!" BOOM! With over 800 people in a packed seminar, this man knew me, remembered what I did, took the time to 'touch' me with … yes, it's true: winsome words.

As to getting help in a big way, that also is a reason why you read this: James Malinchak inspired me with a 'you can do this' message. Truth. The three 10-hour days of learning I spent in December 2015 at James Malinchak's Big Money Speaker conference were 30 of the best hours I've invested in myself, ever. I am a student of what I affectionally, and with admiration, call 'showmen'. So often, these people are speakers, presenters, and charismatic leaders. James Malinchak is all of those. In fact, he is up there with P.T. Barnum, the entrepreneur circus giant portrayed by Hugh Jackman last year in the hit movie *The Greatest Showman*. James knows how to bring the most inspiring and amazing people into an arena and let them WOW the crowd. James is an incredible ringmaster bringing it all together. His workshops, seminars, and especially his private coaching have grown dreams into giant realities for so many speakers, authors, coaches, and businessmen.

Solutions. Be a solutioneer. James helped me and helps thousands of people as he truly lived out the winsome "S" as to 'be a Solutioneer'. He pours his energy and ideas into people to help them realize that they are capable of great things, and that when you believe it, start acting like it, and use his tools, ideas, and coaching, and you will begin to 'walk winsome' in the endeavor that you have dreamed about. Without James Malinchak, you would not be reading this book.

CHAPTER 6

THE "O" FOR OPTIMISM

Of all the letters in the anagram of WINSOME, this "O" is probably the easiest to tag or assume. Optimism. A winsome person simply walks with a profound optimism that things are going to be okay, even better than we might imagine. The 'O' of Winsome is for "BE OPTIMISTIC

> **Dictionary.com defines optimism as:**
>
> 1. a disposition or tendency to look on the more favorable side of events or conditions and to expect favorable outcome.
>
> 2. the belief that good ultimately predominates over evil in the world.
>
> 3. the belief that goodness pervades reality.

The history of the word optimism is to mean "the greatest good". It stems from the Latin word *optimus* "the best". Children and parents who have enjoyed the *Transformers* movies of the last decade will remember Optimus Prime, the lead good Transformer character who was positive, caring, most powerful, and 'the best' of the good guys.

So, as you read this chapter, it might encourage for you a 'transformation' day. You can be the positive, optimistic, powerful person in your circle of life by being the 'Optimus Prime' of your world. Be the WINSOME character around you. Care. Share. Be positive. Look for good. See the good around you. Discover the incredible and extraordinary around you.

We walked through the 'Willing, Interested, Nurturing, and Solutioneering' concepts of WINSOME. Now, let's talk about the one that is, perhaps, the most natural… Optimism.

We are a nation that projects a fast-paced, often high-demand and high-challenge society. It seems we hardly ever rest or relax like we should. That can be so important.

So, let's do that right now. Set down this book. Close your eyes. Sit quietly. Roll your shoulders. Roll your neck. Take a deep breath. Quietly out loud say to yourself five times, "To be winsome is to be able to relax, pause, see good, and be optimistic." Or let's shorten it. "Winsome is relaxing, seeing good, and being optimistic!" Even right now as you're at this stage of the book, you are indeed feeling more optimistic that you're on your way to walking winsome.

Across the globe today, there are over 2,500 Optimist International clubs. I strongly suggest you join one. The first club I ever joined, even as a college student was the Optimist Club. My fraternity pledge father, and the 'Serial CEO' Tom Henning I wrote about in our earlier chapter, recommended it. Optimist Club was yet another building block in my walking winsome.

Optimist clubs often meet only once a month. Their heart is for serving youth and community. They are comprised of local individuals who shape the goals and recipients of the local club's efforts. It might just be the catalyst to greater things ahead for you!

Today in America, community service and community connection is a dying spirit. That, my winsome friends, is a passion that the 'busyness' of our lives has seemed to lessen, and we, the winsome, must rekindle it.

So go check a club near you at visit their website at: www.optimist.org and discover a newfound heart and appreciation for community spirit. Plus, who doesn't want to heed the creed and messages of Optimists International?

Optimist International has a clear mission, vision, and purpose.

> **Mission:**
> By providing hope and positive vision,
> Optimists bring out the best in kids.

> **Vision:**
> Optimist International will be recognized worldwide as the premier volunteer organization that values all children and helps them develop to their full potential.

> **Purposes:**
> To develop optimism as a philosophy of life, utilizing the tenets of the Optimist Creed; to promote an active interest in good government and civic affairs; to inspire respect for the law; to promote patriotism and work for international accord and friendship among all people; to aid and encourage the development of youth, in the belief that the giving of one's self in service to others will advance the well-being of humankind, community life, and the world.

Optimism is, indeed, a key to the enduring spirit of being winsome. Optimism says that you are willing and interested in making yourself and others have a better life. That through your nurturing and solutioneering of each person and situation that arises, you can walk forward, believing and trusting that by God's hand and using the God-given talents you possess, good things are ahead.

I have referenced Optimists International quite a bit here, because I truly have seen and experienced the investment in community, youth, and people that they make. Before I share with you more about how your winsome way will include optimistic ways, I'll share the Optimist Creed.

The Optimist Creed

Promise Yourself

*To be so strong that nothing can
disturb your peace of mind.*

*To talk health, happiness, and prosperity
to every person you meet.*

*To make all your friends feel that
there is something in them.*

*To look at the sunny side of everything
and make your optimism come true.*

*To think only of the best, to work only
for the best, and to expect only the best.*

*To be just as enthusiastic about the success
of others as you are about your own.*

*To forget the mistakes of the past and press
on to the greater achievements of the future.*

*To wear a cheerful countenance at all times and
give every living creature you meet a smile.*

*To give so much time to the improvement of yourself
that you have no time to criticize others.*

*To be too large for worry, too noble for anger,
too strong for fear, and too happy to permit
the presence of trouble.*

Next to being winsome, probably the most common compliment I receive —and I always take it as a big-time compliment— is that I am an eternal optimist. It is true. I do see the glass overflowing in the future, even when it is half full. Even when it's empty, I just know that the glass will be full again one day. I will find a way to fill it up.

Being an optimist or a pessimist can simply be viewed as the way you talk to yourself about the world, your own life, and other people. Optimists often believe in God or a higher power that truly wishes the best for them. They often are found to believe that their own actions result in positive things happening. That they are responsible for or have a strong influence on what's going on in their life and around them. That happiness and joy is just around the corner, if not already present. You can be this way, too!

One goal of this book is for you to expect good things to happen in the future for you and your life. And importantly, for your children, friends, associates, or anyone you can have your winsome way impact.

Optimists don't worry (much). If they *do* worry, they use the worry to review what happened and how to learn from it.

Sadly, pessimists— who will often call themselves 'realists'— think the opposite way. They anticipate bad things or that things are probably not going to be worth the risk. Sometimes, they blame themselves for the bad things that happen in their lives and think that one failure, stumble, or mistake means more will probably inevitably follow. Pessimists see positive events— or even positive, winsome people, like you— as flukes that are outside of their control. That somebody optimistic or winsome is just on a lucky streak. They often might wish for another to stumble.

Let me say this. I have had many pessimistic-leaning friends, co-workers, church members, and people around me. They often help temper my eternal optimism to at least think through my exuberance. In my chapter on the "M" of WINSOME, I will speak to a great friend who, while not really a pessimist, does take an extremely cautious walk into my ideas. And that can be good.

Generally, I find I don't hang out with pessimists, and right now I suggest you review, weigh, and evaluate your closest ten friendships. If you have more than one or two who lean pessimistic, then talk to them about it. Share that you are working in your life to walk winsome and that who we surround ourselves with can often shape our spirit for our own success and happiness, as well as how we impact others. If they, as a close friend, aren't happy for you that you're working to improve and grow and want to help others through the winsome way coaching, then maybe – and I say this respectfully – you need to find another upbeat and optimistic friend.

I have always believed the two keys to friendship are to have a friend who is there to listen, encourage, support, and be a sounding board first. Second and equally important is that when faced with a major situation in your life that true friend will tell you what you need to hear, and not just be a yes man or yes woman who just goes along with you and does not care enough to speak to your heart and mind when needed. We all need friends who tell us what we need to hear and that feels so good. Ask your friends – and we will talk later about your "Winsome Seven Friends" – to give you the truth, when needed.

Gas Station Attendant Millionaire – Larry Scott

My part-time job my last two years at the University of Nebraska was working for Avis Rent a Car at the Lincoln Municipal airport. It was a great job for me, as it dealt with meeting the public, being a welcoming voice to the city of Lincoln, and foremost for me as a young, tall, reasonably handsome and girl-crazy guy of 21, my best part of the job was getting to see flight attendants come off the planes on an hourly basis.

As glorious as it sounds, most of my first six months on the job was comprised with cleaning, vacuuming, gassing up, and otherwise prepping the vehicles for the next rental. Pat Vifquain, the Avis Lincoln Airport Manager—and also a very winsome person—was a true stickler about double-checking all vehicles to make sure the 'We Try Harder' slogan of Avis stood enthusiastically for how clean our cars were in Lincoln, Nebraska.

Avis was, indeed, a 'winsome' company, as they worked harder to make the car rental experience a good one. When you're number two, you 'try harder'. And you walk more winsome when possible, in order to rise to the best you can be. Avis did that.

Thus, many times a day, I drove the returned rentals from the airport to Airport Standard, our partner in the car rental make ready. I'll never forget my first week driving into Airport Standard. Keep in mind that 'full service' gas stations were still in operation, and Airport Standard was, indeed, the best. Each time, I was greeted by someone who would shout at my window, "Good mornin'! Welcome to Airport Standard!"

Before you could get the car window even rolled down, this was belted out enthusiastically by an energetic gentleman in his mid-thirties by the name of Larry Scott. Without any doubt, Larry Scott, the owner of Airport Standard, is one of the most 'winsome' people I have ever known. To this day, even now, in his 70s, Larry's love and motivation for a happy conversation keeps bringing me back to him. He is one of my 'Winsome Seven'.

Larry Scott's philosophy is simple.

> "Make them feel like they are the Number One driver in America, each and every visit to our station."

Larry Scott, the energetic gas station owner and secret millionaire, lived out his method of 'being optimistic' by his boundless energy, enthusiasm and gusto for life, people, and travelers and their cars.

Larry was known by all in the Lincoln area, as well as regular drivers on I-80, as the best place to stop for gas. Larry created the 'experience' concept decades before Starbucks made it famous. Airport Standard was an experience. It didn't matter that his gas signs out front were twenty cents higher and that people knew 'self-serve' was cheaper than 'full service'. He built the most winsome gas and service station in America (that's my story, and I'm sticking to it). Larry and all of us under his coaching not only exuded positivity and optimism, but really believed and wanted drivers to come pay more for gas, but we would change lives for each customer with the spirit, energy, and memory-making moments at Airport Standard in Lincoln. For sure, Larry Scott changed my life. Have you ever watched someone who is enthusiastic about their life, business, or hobby? The look on their face is brilliance. They literally shine. If not for people like Larry Scott, you would not be reading this book. His eternal and overflowing optimism— again, remember he was simply running a gas station— led me into a forever for life belief that whatever your job, role, situation, or arena, do it with enthusiasm above and beyond what people expect. Larry Scott was absolutely a man who woke up and knew he would 'Be Optimistic' and so positive that thousands of drivers would stop because they remembered his winsome nature.

Needless to say, Larry's gusto for life brought him to see something in me he liked, and he offered me a job in the summer months, as I stayed in Lincoln. The 'winsome' concepts of Larry's life impacted me tremendously and from what I gleaned just by being around this tremendous mentor, I was changed.

Small Town USA Leadership – Greg Scholz

Mayor. Postmaster. Fire chief. Any of those three titles, alone, would lend exceptional credibility and honor to any person holding even one of those titles. Imagine holding all three in a community! My lifelong winsome friend Greg Scholz is a small-town champion. Greg's tall, lean, and upbeat presence would light up any room. And for you reading this, remember that if you enter a room looking for friends and for something positive to happen, like Greg always did, you will find it. If you're from a town of less than 25,000 people, this story could especially change your life and your community!

I first came across this tall, confident and talented leader in the fifth grade, as his small-town grade school, Bellwood, Nebraska, played our David City St. Mary's team. Greg, like I was, was the tallest on his team.

Our Catholic school team all laughed at the Bellwood Broncos, because they all wore red kneepads to match their red and white uniforms. We were cool in our Notre Dame colors, of course. Our uniforms were the best. You would not catch us wearing kneepads.

Little did we know that those Bellwood Broncos kneepads were for outhustling and diving to the floor for loose balls and ways to win with all-out heart. And they did most of the time. Greg and I would move into high school and become great friends and study mates, and we both held the title of class president. I was class president our freshman year, then, the class wised up, and Greg was senior class president. To this day, he organizes fun reunions. If you have a classmate like this, do a winsome thing right now, and pick up the phone and call your high school friend. Tell them you are reading a book (and I say with a smile that it might be a good idea to jump on Amazon.com and order them one, too) and that book said to call an old classmate to celebrate and share a WCM with them. A key part of my friendship with Greg was basketball. We made it a tradition to become pre-game layup partners. Athletes can often hold a lot of superstition. In this case, it was true. When there were the few times we weren't layup partners, the game's events seemed to have something down happen. Like a cold March night in Fremont, Nebraska during district basketball finals.

I remember that game our senior year when Greg's knee blew out, and he went down. We were both under the basket, going for the rebound. I'll never forget the pop noise one of his tendons made when it snapped. His entire kneecap came loose and moved well off the center of his knee. It was like a slow-motion movie as he went down, writhing and crying out in pain. As he was to his hometown of Bellwood, Greg was a truly inspirational part of our team. As he lay on the floor awaiting a stretcher, and I was kneeling with Coach Dale Kerkman next to him, Greg's tremendous humor and winsome lighthearted spirit shined through. He looked at me and said, "Do you think this will get me more kisses from the cheerleaders?"

To those who grew up loving music from the group Chicago, you know that one of their songs that was often played at sporting events is the song "25 or 6 to 4". It was the song we did pre-game warmups to. And to this day, when it comes on the radio, either Greg or I will call each other, and if the other one doesn't pick up, we'll play the song on their voicemail.

A key part to take away about being winsome is the "O" of winsome which is 'Be Optimistic'. Be sure you remain optimistic in the relationships you value, and they will last a lifetime.

CHAPTER 7

THE "M" FOR MINDFUL

> **The dictionary definition of mindful is:**
>
> attentive, aware, or careful,
>
> noting or relating to the psychological
>
> technique of mindfulness

The Bible speaks of the renewing of the mind in Romans 12:2, as Scripture shares:

> *"And do not be conformed to this world, but be transformed by the renewing of your mind, so that you may prove what the will of God is, that which is good and acceptable and perfect."*

And when our minds wander to doubt, fear, discouragement, temptation, or areas of thinking we should seek to guard against, Scripture shares to "take captive every thought."

In 2 Corinthians 10:5 with understanding that our human imagination sometimes takes many people to fear and worry, we are encouraged:

> *"Setting aside our imaginations, and every obstacle or presumption that sets itself against the knowledge of God, we should take captive every thought…"*

So how does a winsome person in the spirit of being mindful take thoughts captive? That's a great question that each of us should explore. It's HUGE! We are often faced with a natural tendency, despite few people acknowledging it, to be fearful or cautious, and it often stops or slows us from achieving success, relationships, income, happiness, or reaching our potential. Those are the very thoughts that we should consciously work to lasso and capture them and say 'no' to. To not let negativity and self-doubt get the best of you, but to let the best of you shine forth, and for you to capture those negative thoughts and lock them away as "stinkin' thinkin'".

For me, I must admit that I heard the FUD voices— Fear, Uncertainty and Doubt voices— that said, "You don't have a message and will never write a book." Through people like Zig Ziglar, Bob Sherwood, Bob Beaudine, and many, many others, I was encouraged. Those types of 'winsome' people are exactly who you should be speaking to on a daily basis. These people wanted me to let my light shine bright.

You, too, should know, you may have a book inside you. I truly hope reading this book helps launch a new winsome you that shouts out from deep inside of you, "I can do this!"

It has been proven that positive affirmations do have an impact, if used in a genuine and reasonable methodology. There is a new science and I believe reasonable approach to teaching and coaching people to actively change their thinking and change their life. The understanding of the human brain, how we can re-train or 're-script' our brain as we take our negative thoughts and move them to positive thoughts is a growing concept.

Being mindful encompasses everything from our faith in God, to psychology, to the modern understanding of the brain and its function. The "M" for 'BE MINDFUL' is, for me, probably the most important letter of the 'WINSOME' acronym. Not because I am good at it, but because I am not. In my 60 years of life, I have discovered that to 'know thyself' is key.

A historic Greek figure, Socrates, set forth that timeless phrase, "To know thyself is the beginning of wisdom." Certainly, Socrates will bear up greater than I for centuries to come, yet he wasn't always the winsome fellow he should have been. While I must claim that I received the grade of C+ in my Greek history studies at my beloved alma mater of Nebraska, I do recall learning that Socrates often heard 'voices' and was often questioned as to his thinking.

As to the 'voices' you hear, I can only recommend that God, your spouse, your parents, your closest friends who genuinely have your best interest at heart, are the 'voices' you listen to. Be mindful of those who truly care and those who do not want you to succeed or soar and fully use the God-given abilities you've been given. Be mindful of who you are, what you were made for, and the extraordinary value you possess.

Importantly and with excitement for all of us, the understanding of neurology I spoke of earlier is exponentially growing. We are learning how to re-program and re-script the human mind and change our thinking from our current state to a more winsome way of thinking. Thus, this chapter on being 'Mindful' covers many areas of science, relationships, self-knowledge, and self-discovery.

I smile and share that I do believe *The Winsome Way* could become one of our next generation's iconic books. Spoken humbly, yet with the life lesson and point that if you are going to write a book, teach a course, share a vision, then you sure enough should believe it will test time in 'having legs' and lasting for years to come. You have such timeless and winsome value in you, and thus, this book is in your hands. Something inside you leaped and said, "Buy this winsome book!"

So let's take a WCM, a Winsome Celebration Moment, and celebrate YOU! Set this book down now. Speak out loud what you believe you were born to do. God and your inner passion continue to whisper it, so let's trust that prompting. By doing this daily, you will re-script and re-program your brain with better, stronger, higher purpose-driven 'code'. A code that is winsome and dynamic.

Importantly in this "M" for 'Be Mindful' chapter, in order to serve, encourage, and exhort you, I must challenge and submit to you that you should study personality types and traits. If you have not already, do so. There are a lot of books, online tests, and studies worth exploring. Many take less than 20 minutes to take. Often, they'll bring a smile, a chuckle, and a 'hey, that is me' as you read the outcome of the tests. Do this in the next 90 days, so you'll better recognize your personality traits, strengths, and weaknesses. That, my new winsome friends, is important. It will make you even more winsome.

Too many of us— and I did this myself— became pigeon-holed or pointed to careers or jobs for all the wrong reasons. That's why truly part of this book is for the self-understanding to understand where and by doing what we can best show our 'winsome self'. Know thy strengths, and find a career, passion, hobby, and purpose that encompasses that strength, and you'll maximize your winsomeness.

I shared a lot about strengths above, yet it's also important to know our weaknesses. Each of us has weaknesses. Don't beat yourself up with these. Instead, lift yourself up where you can after you discover them, and use them to help you be mindful of how to move forward with greater success.

> **I would say there are the 'Seven A's of Winsome Mindfulness'**
>
> 1) Aware of your strengths.
>
> 2) Aware of your shortcomings.
>
> 3) Aware of people who want to support and champion you.
>
> 4) Aware of negative people around you.
>
> 5) Aware of your potential.
>
> 6) Aware of needing a coach.
>
> 7) Aware that God is in control.

Later, as I have mentioned, I'll speak about having a 'Winsome Seven'. Amongst your 'Winsome Seven', I hope you are blessed with a friend who will share with you your areas needing attention, show you your blind spots, challenge you to grow out of a bad habit or work through a trait that is not helping you be all you can be.

My winsome friend Bernie, who I spoke of earlier, is truly a person who has always been part of my mindfulness. He is that kind of friend you need. One who loves you enough to tell you what you need to hear, not just what you want to hear.

A challenge in writing this book is that my mind gets distracted often. Some say it is a gift of being quick, that I'm observant of all around me, excited about my surroundings, and often compliment or encourage with exuberance often. That can also be called ADD. Smiling, I have been tested, and what a gift I have! I am borderline ADD, and that allows me to be more creative, energetic, and child-like as I see the world, and child-like qualities, my friends, are part of the definition of winsome. My winsome friend Bob Sherwood also says that if I do have ADD, it is a special trait that helps me be a better coach, mentor, business analyst, and marketer. I see things that others don't. I imagine things that other don't.

NOW, foremost to stay in the winsome way path, I channel that hyper mind activity to who I can help.

That's the message for YOU. Whether you are 5 or 55 years old and have been told 'you are ADD'— or even if you have the appearance of ADD— you should celebrate that. If you've been given this book as a child who has ADD or you've heard me speak on it and something inside you leaped with 'he's like me!', then we've both blessed each other. Not because you and I share these qualities of the ADD/ADHD mindset, but because you should know the awesome qualities of ADD/ADHD and be 'mindful' of their strengths that you possess. Celebrate these qualities.

Extremely intelligent	Adaptable to change
Energetic	Visionaries or dreamers
Humble	Resilient
Hardworking	Athletic
Imaginative	Creative
Fun-loving	Humorous
Very optimistic	Upbeat
Insightful	Very visual
Trusting	Open-minded
Deeply compassionate	Empathetic
Artistic	Passionate
Sensitive	Verbally advanced
Charismatic	Enthusiastic

Quickly then, to add my fellow ADD / ADHD new friends to the list below of some significant people. Here's a list of just a few of these very famous people who used their high energy and creativity to become exceptionally successful people in their respective areas of life. Think about it. What if…? What would our world be like if they had been labeled "problems," held back, repressed, ridiculed, and discounted as troublemakers or a hyperactive problem people who shouldn't be paid attention to? You will see below you're in good company!

Ann Bancroft	Magic Johnson
John Lennon	Michael Jordan
Nostradamus	Babe Ruth
John D. Rockefeller	Eleanor Roosevelt
Beethoven	Mozart
Pete Rose	Louis Pasteur
Napoleon	General George Patton
Pablo Picasso	Steven Spielberg
Harry Belafonte	George Burns
Andrew Carnegie	Dwight D. Eisenhower
Prince Charles	Woodrow Wilson
Einstein	Leonardo DaVinci
Socrates	Galileo
Alexander Graham Bell	Thomas Edison
Orville and Wilbur Wright	F. Scott Fitzgerald
Henry David Thoreau	Edgar Allen Poe
Nolan Ryan	John F. Kennedy
Whoopi Goldberg	Ernest Hemingway
Dustin Hoffman	George Bernard Shaw
Abraham Lincoln	William Randolph Hearst

Today, more and more you can learn about the mind, the brain, and how hormones and electrical stimulus impacts our bodies. Two of the leading champions in the study of the brain are Dr. Daniel Amen and John Assaraf. Their research and studies are fascinating.

I have had the pleasure of meeting and hearing John Assaraf firsthand. His research is detailed and compelling. His message is inspiring and stimulating. Assaraf spoke at a December 2015 Big Money Speaker Boot Camp established years ago by a winsome fellow, James Malinchak, who you read about in the Solutioneer chapter.

Assaraf captivated the audience with his presentation. His opening line made something inside me leap as to my message and your journey toward walking winsome.

> *"Mindset is what separates the rest from the best."*

As John continued on, it struck me what a winsome soul he was, as he freely and openly shared perhaps hundreds of thousands of dollars of time, interviews, and research with our boot camp. He was, indeed, 'willing, interested, nurturing' and for sure was sharing a 'solutions, optimism, mindfulness' as he 'enrolled' us in a better understanding of our potential.

Transformation from where you are at now to a winsome walk through life is what you and I want. As part of the mindfulness of winsome, we must answer another breakthrough question that Assaraf presented to our boot camp.

> *"Are you interested or committed?"*

That's such a key life question. A question for yourself that is important in your quest to walk through life with a more winsome outlook and approach.

It is important to note and encourage others to follow on Social Media or online a national leader in the efforts to encourage authors, speakers, coaches, and seminar professionals, Mr. James Malinchak.

BEING MINDFUL OF YOUR SHORTCOMINGS

Now here is a 'be mindful' moment that happens to me from time to time. I slip from winsome to woesome. What?? Yes, none of us should hold the belief that we can keep a level of winsomeness that we'd like to think we could walk through life with at every moment.

Many times— and I am thankful— people have caught my spirit not being 'winsome' and pointed it out and/or reminded me of it. I'd rather be surrounded by people who'd tell me that than have them go behind my back and say it. Wouldn't you? That's the kind of people, friends, and mentors you should have being a part of your life.

"Dan, I'm not feeling the Winsome here!"

I have a friend named Doug Bachtel. We first met in 2000, when he approached me at a trade show and boldly announced, "So you're the guy that got the job I was looking at. Your boss told me if you fail, I'm in. You're toast," or something to that effect. We smile at that today.

Doug is an exceptionally intelligent and highly analytical person, which is different than my giftedness, as I more often live from gut instinct and feelings.

As Doug is a stickler for detail and process, there have been times when I missed a deadline I'd made with him, or when I got busy and my time slipped away from me and I was late to a non-business phone call, lunch, coffee, or connect time. Or the 'busyness' too often misses caused Doug to utter those words I didn't want to hear, yet needed to hear. "Dan, I'm not feeling the winsome here!"

Ouch. That hit me. Thus, it finds itself here to remind you to be cautious to not make promises or commitments, especially to your friends for life, that you may fail to be able to honor. As we would be perfect and timely when business or money was on the line, make sure that for your relationships, you stay winsome by staying on track and honoring your word. Thanks, Doug Bachtel. And for each of you, right now, stop, set this book down, and call or reach out to someone who had the courage and cared enough to say, "Hey, I'm not feeling the winsome – or respect – from you," and say THANK YOU.

As we wrap up the importance of 'Be Mindful', it is extremely important that you recognize the importance of being mindful of your health. As a nation, a recent study by the Institute for Health Metrics and Evaluation at the University of Washington said that over 70 percent of men and 60 percent of women in America are overweight. Pay attention! Look to your left and look to your right, whether at work, church, the sports stadium, shopping at the mall…wherever and all over… America is overweight.

I shared earlier that by working to be winsome, you will add seven to eleven years to your life by having an optimistic, winsome outlook. Yet, if we don't take care of our health, then all the winsome in the world may not allow us to enjoy people, success, and life like you and I want to. I also speak on fitness, because a key reason in your effort to lead a winsome life and 'be an enroller', indeed, comes with a longer and livelier life.

So, once again, set this book down, stand up, and go to the mirror and shout at the mirror, "Okay! I'm going to be winsome AND healthy!" YES! You can do this.

The Milkman – Bill Eller

As children, we discover that windows lead to outside, which is most often the most fun place to be (contrary to our modern day children, who like to stay inside and play with electronic devices). One of my earliest memories was on Mondays and Thursdays watching for this big, boxy, fancy truck with a cow painted on the side. "The cow truck is here Mommy!" I would shout. This later evolved to, "The milkman! The milkman is here!" Then, it became my twice a week role to greet Bill Eller, the milkman, at our front door and give him the old bottles in exchange for fresh, new milk. After my parents, Bill Eller was, perhaps, winsome model number one. He was always smiling, petting dogs, waving to neighbors, and energetically bounding up our steps to greet my Mom and I. Bill Eller's trademark saying, whether it was a 100-degree day, or freezing cold, or rainy, he'd say, "It's a great day for fresh milk!" Now that's a winsome guy kind of thing to say! Bill frequently gave me a Tootsie Pop or other candy, which, of course, made him a superhero my five-year-old self. As he walked back to his "cow truck", he'd always say, "Drink your milk Danny! Grow up strong!"

I once asked my Mom, "Is there was a cow inside that truck?" Well, that led my mom, who was gifted with a very special talent and creative skill of linking people and moments together, to ask Bill Eller if I could do a 'ride along' some time. (I'm often told today I am a 'Linker' or a 'Connector', so thank you Kitty Snell!) I remember one sunny, spring day when I had become a big boy of five years old, Mr. Eller asked, "Danny, you do such a good job with helping me here at the door of your house, would you like to ride along with me one day?" Boom! That was it! I was 'somebody'! The milkman said I did a great job! He wants *me* to ride along on that cool truck. This was a Super Bowl-sized event, before the Super Bowl had even been thought up! "WOW, YES!" I enthusiastically shouted. I ran and told my Mom, who Bill Eller said I had to ask first. She smiled big, as if knowing nothing, and said, "You must really be a special boy to ride with the milkman."

I only rode with Bill Eller maybe three times, yet I remember the first very early morning. My Mom told me, "You'll want to look good for the houses on the milk run. Let's wear your black pants and white shirt." She even ironed my white shirt. In that early, life-defining moment, I was somebody! I was the milkman's helper! The morning was sunny and warm, yet when the sliding door to the back end was opened, the last of cold air bounced me up to attention. Mr. Eller had already loaded his truck. We were off to deliver. I probably carried over 30 bottles of milk that morning.

Milkman Bill Eller was a person who truly was 'Mindful'. Even in my young days of life, I could see something special about Bill Eller. He was winsome merely by being a positive, cheerful, upbeat, energetic fellow who people saw having a special 'solution': fresh milk and ice cream.

Now who doesn't like fresh milk and ice cream? Of course, Bill Eller was 'Mindful' of the coming change in dairy distribution and that to keep customers, he needed to be extra special. He was winsome because he was mindful his future business was at stake every year. America has lost the days of the milk delivery man, yet some regional homegrown milk farms pop up daily. As part of Bill Eller teaching me how to be mindful of keeping the customers happy, I often got to share a small cup of milk with a homeowner not on his delivery route. Or sometimes, a small cup of Lucerne Ice Cream. Woohoo… one small cup of Lucerne vanilla ice cream, and we'd sell a half gallon out of the truck. And often, Bill Eller was then 'mindful' of the extra attention he'd give them to start them on his delivery route for milk, cream, and ice cream. For Bill, simply being there, being winsome, and offering a product or service people liked kept them using his service. That's something to remember for your world.

Let there be no mistake. Someone in Bill Eller's early life had taught him to be upbeat, friendly, enthusiastic for his work, and effervescent in his service to people. Everybody loved Bill Eller, the milkman. His personality stuck in my brain and registered as good. I learned something from him. You can, too.

The Zig Ziglar of UNL – Dr. Keith Pritchard

When I arrived at the University of Nebraska with my powerful score of 21 on the ACT (thankful the state took me), my goal was to become a high school teacher and basketball coach. I absolutely knew I was one day going to win a championship leading a group of young men to a magic moment and a trophy. I began a curriculum toward such a goal, and one of the classes one had to take was the History and Philosophy of Education. It was a 7:30 a.m. class, which did not particularly align with my nights out until 1 a.m. at the local watering holes. I held a bit of stinkin' thinkin' in that season of my life, which I am not proud of today. More on that later. Dr. Keith Pritchard, from the very first 7:30 a.m. class start that sophomore year September was a life-changer. I had discovered a professor who loved what he did, loved improving lives, loved using 'edutainment' (a word that didn't get invented until the 90s) as a teaching style, and it showed.

Dr. Keith Pritchard enthusiastically moved around the room, engaging the class, prancing from side to side, telling stories on and off the subject, and truly as Zig Ziglar used to say, spoke "at 120 words a minute, with gusts up to 180". Zig published his first book, *See You at the Top*, in 1975. I had just recently seen and heard him in Omaha, as Ziglar was then new to the motivational and inspiration scene. He would go on to become a hero of mine and is often called the "greatest motivational speaker of all time". I said to my friend, yes, my winsome friend Bernie, who also was in the class, that, "Dr. Pritchard reminds me of that Zig Ziglar *See You at the Top* guy." Dr. Pritchard's quick, energetic, and lively southern voice – he had spent years at Wake Forest and the University of Virginia – lit up the classroom. Students loved him.

Keith Pritchard was truly the best college teacher I ever had. Let there be no mistake, he is winsome. He made sure students left his classroom carrying something each day that they would carry forward into the world. He truly paid it forward. Dr. Prichard enriched his classes by his experience, wisdom, and excitement for education. He often cited facts, showed (pre-PowerPoint) statistics and pictures via the then commonly used transparencies projected from the old boxy desktop unit onto a screen. Pritchard would go up and touch the screen and then run to the back of the room saying, "This is the classroom of tomorrow," or some other tip for we future educators. Dr. Pritchard shared with me after class one day when I told him I loved his enthusiasm that people will learn best when they feel someone cares about them and is excited to be with them. I carried that into my business life, sports coaching, family, and church life. It has made for much success.

CHAPTER 8

THE "E" FOR
ENROLLER

> **Dictionary.com says of enroll and enrollment;**
>
> - to write the name of (a person) in a roll or register; place upon a list; register
> - to enlist (oneself)
> - to put in a record; record
> - to roll or wrap up
> - to enroll oneself

Everyone Enrolls Every Day

By the time you finish this chapter, I believe you will see that you are, indeed, an 'Enroller'. If you're not, then you'll hopefully discover a way to be an enroller and understand the importance of 'enrollment'. Because you've been enrolled everyday of your life. It's true. So, start now fully your winsome role and be an enroller!

As I shared the acronym idea with those around me, who immediately suggested some obvious "E" words that I should use for the "E" of Winsome.

Many times, I heard phrases like…

"Dan, you are MR. ENCOURAGEMENT! You have to use ENCOURAGEMENT for the 'E' in Winsome!"

"Dan you are Mr. ENTHUSIASM!"

"You are full of pep in your step and have loads of ENERGY!"

"Dan when you enter the room, you are always immediately ENGAGING the people and the entire room."

"Dan, you create EXCITEMENT about your product or message, so the 'E' has to be about building excitement!"

While I'm honored to be called any or all of those, and absolutely I believe all those qualities—encouragement, energy, engagement and excitement— will add to your life in every way. It is also important to know that while those qualities should be displayed, the timing and appropriate use of them can win or lose the moment. Our discussion of 'be mindful' is important in this scenario.

I first decided that to encourage you to be winsome every day, you should consider working to be the EMBODIMENT of winsome. In other words, fill your mind, thoughts, spirit, and energy with winsomeness, so that you truly represent the word winsome and you are the EMBODIMENT OF WINSOME.

I even began writing preliminarily on that 'be the embodiment' message, until I heard an audio broadcast by Forbes Riley, the award-winning TV host, author, fitness guru, and entrepreneur. Forbes Riley is truly one who has become a brand name by herself. Forbes is one of the nation's leading health and wellness expert and is a recent inductee into the National Fitness Hall of Fame.

You've seen Forbes Riley on TV shows like HSN, the Home Shopping Network, Forbes Living, and other infomercial companies. Riley has appeared in over 120 infomercials, offering a genuine and truly proven pitch about SpinGym or other product. Forbes Riley has sold over $2 billion dollars' worth of product. She is perhaps the #1 'ENROLLER' in America. She 'enrolls' the audience into buying into her fitness or nutritional message.

I first heard Forbes Riley on a podcast speaking about 'enrolling' and engaging people into a message, a fitness program, or any other belief or product you have. She stressed the importance of enrollment and how important it is in every brand name. Riley is nationally recognized not only in fitness, but as being a true guru in how to build a brand. And, indeed, Forbes Riley enrolled me with her energy, enthusiasm, and excitement about her products. Whether she is on stage, on TV, or on the radio, Forbes Riley is truly a WINSOME person.

By the time you finish this chapter, I hope you will come to realize that we are most always in a role where we can say that part of our WINSOME way is that indeed we are able to "BE AN ENROLLER".

Enrollment Begins Moment One of Life.

You certainly don't remember it, but the very moment you arrived on this planet, there was a room full of people working to 'enroll' you into the population of our world. In fact, two people, your mother and father, were, in most cases, the most enthusiastic and excited enrollers of the bunch. That first moment of life, a doctor enrolled you into the world, with the pushing of Mom, probably with the coaching of Dad alongside her. Then, in that very first minute of your life, a pediatric nurse immediately enrolls you into the healthcare system you'll live with all your life by recording your weight, height, respiration, temperature, and other tests, called the APGAR test. Then, the most awaited enrollment for any parent— and it is a miracle moment for any parent— is when the baby is laid upon Mom's chest for the first touch outside the womb. Normally this 'enrollment' moment brings about tears of joy and exuberance. Exuberance is another great "E" word, isn't it?

Next, Dad, or sometimes Grandmother, Grandfather, or a close friend gets to hold YOU! YOU are officially exalted (another "E" word) and clearly seen as the greatest entertainment (Yes another "E") they have ever seen. The moment you enter the world, you become 'enrolled', and your life begins.

Next, you'll get enrolled in your first feeding. Then, you'll enroll in your first meconium bowel movement, (i.e. first poop), which by the way does not stink at all. This may be too much information (LOL), but some don't know that their first poop didn't stink. And it's important to know that if Doctor Oz can say 'poop' on national TV, it's okay for me to write it on a page. I hope you are smiling. If not, then I'll move forward with more of the "be an enroller" message for you as you learn to walk winsome through life. The important thing to take from this is that from moment one of life, we are being enrolled or are then, ourselves, enrolling others.

Week one of life, we enroll our parents, or care providers, into the system of paying attention to us when we need food or have dirty diapers. As a dad, I remember the powerful cries of all our children as they announced to the house that poop or pee was causing discomfort. Quickly, a baby learns 'how to' skills of enrolling.

In early years, we are enrolled by babes to 'pick me up', to 'play with me', to 'help me reach that thing', to 'give me food', or hundreds of other moments where child enrolls family.

Then, life continues and children, most always for growth and betterment are 'enrolled' in daycare, pre-school, youth sports, piano lessons, Boy or Girl Scouts, and thousands of other 'enrollment' moments that parents address each and every week across America.

Fast forward to what's part of enrolling today for you as young adults and upwards in our relationships, teamwork, romantic encounters, workplace, family life, and even every Sunday at church. Each and every one of these, we are either 'enrolling' or 'being enrolled'.

As you walk through life and the older you get, you'll discover that everyone in life has challenges or problems. You are facing challenges. I face challenges. Most people reading this book have heard, as I did early in life, that 'problems are really just opportunities!' Wouldn't it be wonderful if each of us for our specific challenge could be 'enrolled' in a solution to solve our problem? See, the enrolling is that opportunity to grow for all.

I encourage you to always make sure— as integrity is part of a winsome person— that our 'enrolling' efforts are always for a good, positive, honorable, and beneficial purpose of another. For extreme examples, you will not be winsome if you enroll someone to jump off a cliff, run through poison ivy, or even purchase something that does not serve their life. Just use your winsome talent of being an enroller for good.

WINSOME ENROLLMENT PEOPLE STORIES

Style & Enthusiasm - Gary Novotny

It was 1972, and I was the #1 golfer on David City Aquinas golf team. A fellow sophomore from the town of Wahoo, Nebraska, Gary Novotny, was the #1 player on the Wahoo Neumann golf team we were facing on my home course, a course I will smile and refer to as the 'prestigious' David City Golf Club. DCGC was a sand green golf course. Yes, for those of you who may have never heard of such a thing, that means that the actual putting greens were made of sand that was heavily oiled. The winsomeness of Gary Novotny has nothing to do with sand greens, so I challenge you to go to Google and look up sand green golf courses.

Gary Novotny, from the first meeting and the story below, to this day, is a perennial enroller. He engages, connects, convinces and 'enrolls' people in whatever passion he sets before then.

Now to our story that began a lifelong close friendship between two winsome fellows. The first thing I noticed was the colorful golf pants and shirt my opponent had on. I fancied myself as watching my golf legend hero Arnold Palmer enough to make sure I had 'the look' of a champion. Gary had style equal or above mine. He had won the golf apparel points. He also was clearly the team leader, even as a sophomore, and his coach and teammates looked to him for quips, humor, motivation, and even a little taunting. He started by referring to our yellow/golden team golf towels as bananas. My teammates came by me quietly and said, "Take this guy to the woodshed." It was showdown time. Match on!

The first hole was a dogleg to the left, which I birdied and Gary doublebogied. I was up three strokes. Hole two was a short 119 yards over the creek. I took par. Gary hit one long and out of bounds. Took a seven on the par three, and I was up seven strokes after two holes. His plaid pants and cocky bravado from the first tee box turned to humility. Humility is also a winsome quality, which we will touch on in later chapters.

I remember Gary walking over and saying, "I guess God showed me the banana towel comment was not in good taste." We were Catholic high school boys, so frequent reference to the Almighty was natural. We began to laugh and smile, and I put my hand around him and said something about my teammates shouting "Wahoo!" at his misfortune. So, I had struck back with the taunting somewhat, and I believe on that third tee box, a lifetime winsome friendship was born.

The third hole was a long par four. My drive was straight out about 280 yards. Gary sliced his balled to the far right. I was feeling pretty good, and word had spread by now that I was "schooling the cavalier". Both the behavior and the school team mascot was cavalier. As we walked to the far right to look for Gary's ball, we discovered that his ball was about six inches out of bounds. His day and his game were sinking fast. My confidence and my smile were growing bigger.

Now, being then a man who'd learned much of grace and kindness from my parents and numerous nuns at St. Mary's Grade School and Aquinas High, my charitable 'winsomeness' kicked in. I thought that given that I was already seven strokes up, that some degree of (winsome) cheerfulness and kindness might be in order. So, I stepped near his absolutely out of bounds ball, feigning as if looking to make sure it was out of bounds, and I faked a trip and kicked his ball in bounds, saving him going back to hit his tee shot again and two strokes. Are you all smiling at these two sophomore Catholic boys by now? Well, I was Mr. Nice Guy. Certainly, Gary and I look back and laugh together each and every time this story is shared.

So, guess what happens. I birdied the hole. Totally on-fire game. Two birdies in the first three holes. My coach whispered to me as he walked by, "In your face, Novotny." I had gained two more strokes that hole and was now nine strokes ahead after three holes. We were only playing nine holes in the match.

Can you now imagine—as Paul Harvey made famous—'the rest of the story'? Gary proceeded to par out the course. He was the number one golfer on their team for a reason. I totally fell apart, losing ten strokes to him over the next six holes, and you guessed it: Gary won the match by one stroke. The two-stroke penalty – covered by my winsome foot on hole three – would have been the difference. I could not say. To his credit, he wanted to say, knowing the catholic priests who were present as athletic leaders would have potentially gotten us in huge trouble. I believe we refer to such things as 'white lies', which I do not recommend—telling them is not really a winsome quality. Truth is the best. Learn from hole three in David City Golf Club to always tell the truth! Gary Novotny is a world class "ENROLLER"

Championship Heart Builder – Coach Chris Creighton

One of the most exciting football stories of 2016 was Eastern Michigan's turnaround football program, led by one of the most engaging, enthusiastic, and energetic coaches in America: Chris Creighton. Creighton has led the formerly ranked bottom five within NCAA football to two bowl games and winning seasons twice in the last three years. Chris Creighton recruits with heart and passion. He leads and builds winsome young men. Coach Creighton is also an ENROLLER, the last letter in WINSOME. E = ENROLLER.

Chris Creighton recruited my son Lee while Creighton was head coach at Drake University. My son 'enrolled' into the message, inspiration, and program because of Chris Creighton. In Lee's first three years, he collected memory-maker moments via two championships, including diamond-laden Pioneer Conference Championship rings. No one can ever take that away. Coach Creighton enrolled over 150 young men into a program, and he built champions. Enrollers build up people. They look for and see the greatness in people. Being an 'enroller' is a true go forth and walk winsome message.

Enrollment is a powerful word. Each of us takes part in being an 'enroller' every single day, often without even thinking about it. Yes, if you are listening to this, you probably have the type of personality that wants to develop, to grow, to be better today than you were yesterday.

Like Chris does in each of Chris's life passions or relationships, be it his faith, marriage, family, football, neighbors, media, or whatever... we should be enrolling by touches that bear a winsome way nature. Follow Chris Creighton and his winsome style, and I guarantee more daily joy.

To be a successful Enroller, we also should work at having an ENGAGING spirit, holding an ENERGETIC passion for what you believe in, and whatever it is you believe, you want to ENROLL a person into. Foremost—and absolutely a key to any successful enroller—is to deliver your message with ENTHUSIASM!

Hmmm... Doesn't that sound like a coach? Which takes us back to Chris Creighton, Winsome Coach of the Year in 2016 and 2017. He has lived the Winsome Way as an 'enroller' for over 20 years at Ottawa University, Wabash College, Drake University, and Eastern Michigan University. He's been pouring himself into young men and building their characters since the first day he picked up a whistle and a clipboard.

America's Mayor – Rich Becker

I met Lenexa, Kansas Mayor Rich Becker during a political gathering of local officials shortly after I had lost my enthusiastic, yet futile attempt to seek public office as mayor of my city Shawnee, Kansas. I had challenged a six-term, deeply entrenched, and well-known sitting Mayor, and I had finished fifth...out of five people running. Dead last. But the message of my 'Fresh Ideas' candidate was a good one, and seeds were planted in the community. It would pay off. A winsome message that is 'others-focused' always wins the day in the long term.

After a nice newspaper article talking about my energetic, creative, never-seen-before campaign marketing methods, I was sought after by numerous non-profits, who thought they could use the enthusiasm, energy, and style brought to the city in our campaign team.

We signed on with a local food pantry and childcare group and immediately announced that we were going to do a post-election fundraiser: a celebrity roast of the local, just re-elected mayor, Mayor Tony Soetaert for the charity Shawnee Community Services. Someone suggested that who might be better to roast Mayor Soetaert then the neighboring city mayor to the south. So, I approached the mayor of Lenexa, Rich Becker, with the question, "Would you help us and be a roaster?" He beamed his giant smile, and immediately said, "I don't know you, Dan, but I like you already! We'll have lots of fun roasting Tony. Count me in!"

I convinced a local comedian, Calvin Coolidge (yes, named after the President), to be the grand finale roaster. Rich Becker was the roaster right before him. Calvin acknowledged at night's end he should have never followed Rich. Rich had gotten his Lenexa Parks and Recreation Director, Bill Nicks, to write his jokes, and Nicks put together a still-memorable night of one-liners and digs about the two neighboring cities.

Within a week after that roast, I received a call from a mutual friend, Augie Bogina, a self-proclaimed non-winsome guy who fancied himself more like Al Pacino in *The Godfather* as a mastermind in politics. I smile and say that with admiration, as we all have someone we know who would not even want to consider being winsome. For whatever reason that works for them, they develop a style that doesn't seek the benefits of being winsome. Yet the real winners, like Augie, seem to love winsome folks, and he has helped many people, including myself, get elected to public office. Winsome people need 'Godfather' types alongside them. We can't do certain things that they are gifted at.

Before I knew it, Rich Becker was asking me to serve as an out-of-border, outside-the-city planning commissioner for Lenexa. I accepted, and that launched my steps into local politics. A friendship and admiration began in those two weeks that lived mightily on until Rich's death in 2007. Rich would go on to support me in my successful 1989 quest to be a city councilman.

People loved winsome Rich Becker. He told me often, "Hey, hey, remember this, Dan. People want to see their leaders working hard and doing good…and having fun in the process." Rich always led with energy, enthusiasm, a positive outlook, and a 'can-do' spirit. He was known throughout the metropolitan area as a cheerleader extraordinaire for whatever cause he promoted.

He went on to be elected a state representative and, then, as a state senator for his area of Kansas. Later, Rich ran for governor of Kansas. He walked into the county seats of every single county in Kansas: 105 counties. The miles, travel, late nights, poor diet, and passion for that campaign landed him in the hospital, affecting his kidneys, which eventually led to regular dialysis and, later, his death.

I remember the call from Bill Nicks, Jr., regarding his passing. If you've ever lost a mentor and gotten 'the call', you know the slow-motion, sit down, and head down tears that accompany that moment. Truly God had needed a winsome man in heaven. Rich heeded the call.

Rich Becker 'enrolled' me in the local world of Kansas public service, and he is a model for 'enrollment'.

Enrollment as a Profession

I spent 32 years of my life as a salesperson, selling mostly technology, yet also spending time in advertising and the non-profit arena. All professions—even whatever profession you are in right now as you read this—involve you, and ask of you to 'be an enroller'. Whatever we do, we are either enrolling or un-enrolling a person. IBM's Thomas Watson once coined the phrase, "Everybody sells or everybody unsells." This is truth. Enrolling is a partner with selling. Whether you think you "hate salespeople" or not, you, yourself, sell every day. Life is about relationships. You either choose to enroll and invest in relationships or they dwindle. Society, and the divorced and broken families across the country, are the outcome of men, women, relatives, children, and friends not 'enrolling' in the success of the family or marriage.

I submit to you this moment to 'enroll' and engage yourself into a family member, friend, neighbor, classmate, or someone who maybe simply needed someone in their life. Remember, The WINSOME Way is about pouring your life into others. This book does not say, "It's about me, my, or mine." It's about you, we, us, and others. 'Enroll' today in that others-first spirit and pour into another person's life and watch what happens.

The concept of 'enrolling' is one that is fundamental to being winsome. We started our chapter talking about the dictionary meaning of the word. Let's look at that more in-depth.

We started with the meaning of 'enroll' being; to write the name of (a person) in a roll or register, or also to put in a record.

As you're reaching the end of reading this book, and seeking to be winsome, I'm hoping you will have gleaned information and ideas how you might grow your relationships, connections, success, and business. You'll often do so by 'writing the name in the roll of your mind' of a person or organization with a deeper level of connection. You are 'registering' or 'recording' them as closer to you, more connected and comfortable, thanks, we hope, to your new winsome skills.

Then, there is the concept of your own winsome growth by you doing the process of your own 'enrollment' into something that will help you grow or shine brighter in whatever your personal or professional arena. You might enroll in a class, a workshop, or even take part in ongoing Winsome Coaching via our amazing 'Winsome Triple Team' approach to coaching. In any event… walking winsome becomes a habit.

CHAPTER 9
FIVE WINSOME COMPANIES

Winsome people naturally make others feel good. They make us smile. They lift our spirits. We naturally want to be around them. That's our goal for this book. To build your own 'winsome way' in your personality, both personally and professionally.

On our website, we have a monthly poll for winsome companies. We let people vote for the companies that shine bright. Companies that want and strive to be there. In America today, there are many companies who it could be said of, "This organization has a winsome way about them." I have seen many in my travels. I'm sure you have, too. You know them. Something about the spirit of the organization. They put pep in the step of their employees. The cheerful greeting, an extra effort, work hard and have fun, while holding an optimism of a 'can-do' atmosphere.

So, before I share my current "FAB FIVE" winners with whom I've experienced the personal and family delights by their winsome behavior, let's explore YOUR THREE to FIVE top companies you would say are winsome.

1. _____
2. _____
3. _____
4. _____
5. _____

Now… think on this for a moment. What if you were to go tell these companies that you're reading a book and you listed them as one of your picks for a 'winsome' company. Do you think you'd be pouring positive feeling about themselves into their life? Absolutely. Do you think they'd probably share with other employees or teammates that you, (fill in your name here), are a special customer or client and just listed them as winsome? They may even ask, "What is winsome?" Then, you get to spread the winsome way around America a little bit. How about you! You are a winsome movement leader!

SOUTHWEST AIRLINES, MARRIOTT BONVOY, WELLS FARGO BANK, STARBUCKS and KRONOS

The Reigning Winsome Five in Corporate America Today

In my 30+ years of traveling America and the world, there have been five companies in the 'service' industry that stood out. One I had the privilege to work for, Kronos.

Foremost and naturally, I love upbeat, positive, winsome people. Keep in mind my life model stemmed a lot from Larry Scott, who ran a gas station in Lincoln, Nebraska and still is my go-to reflection of how to make a customer number one. You can tell a lot about the corporate training department in the first 60 seconds of encountering these companies.

Leadership, culture, and for sure a 'winsome way' begins at the top of a training or leadership development team, and these five training teams get thumbs up winsome kudos from me as to their winsome teams. I am an expert and study winsome people and companies.

Southwest Airlines

I have never met a person who doesn't smile when they think of or speak of Southwest Airlines. I sat alone at a Kansas City International Airport Starbucks recently on a Saturday morning. I asked people after they got their coffee about Southwest Air. I asked twenty-two people in one hour. Twenty had instant smiles. Sixteen had fun stories from a trip. Three people—including a businesswoman just back from Dallas and two entrepreneurs just back from California— all had stories of singing flight attendants. Only two people had not been on a Southwest flight. They did remember that Southwest ads were fun, and they didn't charge for baggage, so they would "probably fly Southwest one day". Can you imagine any business getting such kudos from 22 people in just an hour? Out of the blue. Founder and the late CEO Herb Kelleher is an America Dream story. He is also the founder of what I call the "Most Winsome Fare in the Air". I took my first flight on Southwest Air in 1978, and today, I still look first to the airline that epitomizes winsome flying… Southwest Airlines. #WinsomeCompany #TheMostWinsomeFareInTheAir

Marriott Bonvoy

I am a lifelong believer and a student of "give a smile, get a smile." I always stay at a Marriott, unless one is not available nearby. That is rare, as Marriott—now coupled with Sheraton—is a lodging organization that takes from top to bottom a winsome approach to building properties and, foremost, staffing properties that serve from the highest of incomes in the world to middle income families. In 2018, I traveled and stayed almost 100 nights at Marriott properties. Because I look for that Marriott staff smile and engagement, I can enthusiastically share that, at each and every property, in 2018, I received a warm smile each and every time I approached the front desk. That— and very clean and up-to-date properties—keeps me coming back.

> *"Remember that a person's name is to that person the sweetest and most important sound in any language."*
>
> *~ Dale Carnegie*

Dale Carnegie is an iconic American author, speaker, and motivator, and is known to have coined that phrase first. *How to Wins Friends and Influence People* was the first book I read that began to shape my life and is second only behind Zig Ziglar's *See You at the Top* as having an impact in how I think. Carnegie is buried in Belton, Missouri. After discovering that, I am working to launch the annual 'Dale Carnegie' America Awards" in Cass County, Missouri. America will come to the heartland to honor this legend. We honor people, companies, teams, and events that exemplify the Carnegie way of thinking.

Wells Fargo Bank

As I shared early on, my father was a banker. He knew how to listen, explore, share, care, and in every way be a winsome banker to the people of Butler County, Nebraska. As a lifelong Winsomeologist—even before I invented the term—I was able to study and learn early in life by watching my dad be the leading banker in the region and even known throughout the state. I saw banking at its finest.

Wells Fargo Bank, which is now the seventh financial institution I've used since my twenties, and by far the most the bank that, like my hometown bank, most closely aligns with the winsome way of doing business. I have found their staff, their engaging way of customer care at their facilities, and their ever-present electronic means of 'touching' their customers to be the finest in the land. Wells Fargo is the most winsome bank in America, bar none. Also, they get kudos for their ongoing and admirable comeback story. Facing a challenge head on.

One of the attributes we have learned in this book is that the "M" stands for "be Mindful." Someone reading this might try to note and remind me of the stumbles that Wells Fargo has experienced due to a small number of people making poor choices. I understand that people were hurt. Improper accounts were opened. I've also learned to not instantly judge and to watch for the process of resolution to come out. I have seen multiple full-page ads and commercials produced that gave me enough trust that the leadership and the board of Wells Fargo have maintained a winsome way of working to rebuild their image. I believe one of the most encouraging comeback ads I've seen in decades. I'm reminiscent of Lee Iacocca with the famous 'The New Chrysler Corporation' when the Chrysler automobile product line was close to losing the public's buying interest.

Frankly, how one perceives the Wells Fargo "Re-Established" campaign, where they share their history and their heart to grow back, depends on everyone's life. If you've faced adversity. If you were down and tried to make a comeback. If you've faced public or even media spotlight and questions. As for me, I've been there. I feel the collective pain, and I also believe their genuine desire to share. "Born 1852, re-established 2018." I love that theme and applaud the Wells Fargo leadership for taking on the damage, admitting to it, and setting for a plan to 're-establish'. That is part of being a winsome company.

One of their commercials speaks the bank's origins in the Old West, in the 19thcentury, as a trusted carrier of gold and other goods by stagecoach. It notes that, "We always found the way; until we lost it," which is a reference to the bumps they faced in recent years. Growing up a Midwest small town young cowboy wannabe and fan, of course I connect with the heritage. Then the spot shared, "It's a new day at Wells Fargo." The ads speak to hearts and express how Wells Fargo is fundamentally a different company today and that it will continue to improve. "While we've made solid progress, we recognize there is still work to be done."

To me, and I hope to you, as a reader, how you handle a 'storm' speaks to your character. Wells Fargo shines in a winsome way to me, and I am the Winsomeologist. So, there we go!

Starbucks Coffee

While I've never met Howard Schultz, the former CEO and entrepreneurial legend at Starbucks, the thing I admire most about what Starbucks created was what's been called "The Starbucks Experience". That's why I believe they are a winsome company and why, as a Winsomeologist, I salute their passion toward serving their customers and creating a destination where people feel great and appreciate the hands-on interest in pleasing their wishes. Serving others. How many times have you read that in this book? A lot. Starbucks is a place where people gather and know it's going to be a positive time.

Joseph Michelli, who wrote 'The Starbucks Experience' notes that the company trains their employees in key three areas. How to 'connect, discover and respond'. Three very winsome principles for sure.

Kronos

There is a great saying 'People won't remember what you did, but they'll remember how you made them feel'. I worked for Kronos. And by far it is the finest organization I've ever worked for in all my years of professional selling. And even today, 91% of Kronos employees say it is a "great place to work". While the first four companies also excel with their employees, Kronos holds many reasons that garner them my "Winsome Company" award, and not just because they were great to work for 20 years ago but how they show up today. Kronos, in 2019, continues to be award-winning and ranked as: Fortune Top 100 Company to Work For, 'Best Workplaces for Millennials' and 'Best Workplaces for Technology'. When a company has employees that work with zeal and gusto – what I'd call a 'winsome heart' – it filters down to the customers and clients. Clients 'feel' the positivity and then benefit from that because of the inspired hearts of the Kronos team to serve them.

The Kronos winsome way 'make them feel' they are important, valued and always the reason Kronos exists. It we that way when I was there, and it remains that way today. I still visit my Kronos clients 20 years later and they still use Kronos. A legacy I'm proud of as a professional salesperson.

Importantly, and unrelated to Kronos but to your winsome walk through life. Stay in touch with your old clients and you'll discover the joy in friendships like you wouldn't imagine. Pick up and call an old client as you read this right now. Do it. They'll feel great. You'll feel great. Try it. Let me know what happened.

Aron Ain, the CEO of Kronos, rose up the ranks over his time. He was climbing the corporate ladder and merely held a senior leadership position when I was a sales rep. So, when a heartland of America kid who was just one of many on the 'club' trip said hello, Aron engaged and asked all about me, my family, my territory and my greatest deal I'd sold. Foremost I remember at that moment we were on a scuba diving boat in Hawaii, a perk of success as we had earned 'Legend Makers' (President's Club) status. My hobby was photography. Aron had his camera and we spent over an hour talking photography. I still have a picture of the CEO of Kronos and me. I cherish it as today that man holds the top office of a very 'winsome company'.

CHAPTER 10
YOUR WINSOME SEVEN

> *I think it's important to get your surroundings as well as yourself into a positive state - meaning surround yourself with positive people, not the kind who are negative and jealous of everything you do.*
>
> Heidi Klum

So you've finished for the most part the appetizers and the main course of this meal we call 'The Winsome Way'. Now, the best-tasting part, which will come next, is the dessert of the program. The part that you should say is the part of the program that truly brings the best memory. It is your "Winsome Seven".

In the very early pages this book, I spoke of my winsome friend, Bob Beaudine. Remember, Bob is the author of *The Power of Who* and most recently, his bestselling *Two Chairs*.

Bob often uses the acronym "YAWYAW", standing for "You Are Who You Associate With". The Winsome Seven absolutely echoes that. My friend, author, speaker, and coach Dr. Dan Erickson and his latest book, *Ready to Soar*, is all about surrounding yourself with people of faith, character, success, and enthusiasm if it's your goal to have success and be a person of faith and character. Both of these mighty men are part of my Winsome Seven for a reason. These two men are absolutely two of the most encouraging, straight-talking, challenging, and caring people I know. After I see them or talk to them, I am immediately lifted, pumped up, and also challenged to do more than I thought I could do prior to our time together. I love that! Do you have people right now in your life like that? I trust if you do, your life is reflecting solid, steady progress.

If you don't, then today is YOUR DAY. Today is the day that you launch a new season of winsome fellowship. You will find seven people whom you can pour your newfound winsome way into, as well as have a hunch that they will want to lift you up in return. And with that, launch a new season of life, progress, attitude, success, and self-fulfillment. Keep this in mind as you select your Winsome Seven. You may change your lineup from time to time. For whatever reason, you'll stay close, but the weekly commitment to each other must be there. Often, you may even move, change jobs, or join a group, church, or club that allows you a new, special, winsome opportunity. Yes, even a group that you are particularly connected to can be like a 'person'. A group like a Rotary Club, a community sports team, like a softball or bowling team you play on, or a women's or men's bible study, or a church fellowship can and should at least serve for one of your days from your Winsome Seven. I'll explain below.

What is the mutual stake in the ground for your Winsome Seven?

> *Five easy steps to the weekly call or connection you'll make.*
>
> 1) Remind them weekly how important they are.
>
> 2) Share the best and worst moments of the week.
>
> 3) Highlight their best moments and lift them up for their worst.
>
> 4) Remind them of the SPECIALNESS that makes them WINSOME.
>
> 5) Share a special quote, theme, story, message, or idea for the week.

So that you can understand the concept of the Winsome Seven, let me share with you my own seven, so that you might feel and see a 'how to' and an example of the winsome power and mighty boost that's in store for you.

WINSOME SEVEN SUNDAY:

Most people think our week begins with Monday. Yet Sunday is the most important day of your life. For many reasons, it should serve as a true winsome day. Sundays are traditionally a time to rest, recharge, regroup your family, health, spirit, and energy. Remember I said that a member of your Winsome Seven can be a group? Well, FAMILY can and should be a part of your Winsome Seven. Why? Because if you regularly invest time, heart, and energy as you pour interest, encouragement, nurturing, help with solutioneering of problems, encouraging optimism, being mindful of everyone's spirit, time, and situations, and, then, enrolling the family into each other's wellbeing, then, the FAMILY WINS! And a family that spends time, prays, eats supper, listens, and encourages one another is for sure a WINSOME FAMILY!

A couple of important thoughts about the 'supper table'. The supper table is the biggest character-building, nation-shaping, and inspirational opportunity missed in America today.

Dr. Ken Canfield, founder of The National Center for Fathering and a 2006 candidate for Governor of Kansas took the 'supper table' message to the people of Kansas. A total unknown in politics, Canfield almost won. Why? Because part of his campaign was gathering Kansans in towns big and small around kitchen tables. As his campaign manager, I coined the phrase for him to use, "Most of the problems of Kansans are not so big that we can't solve them around a kitchen table." It resonated. It had legs. It sold. Canfield rose from sixth in the primaries to tied for first, before the newfound tradition of negative politics rose up and cost him the race. Yet the "kitchen table" message will stand long after his one-and-done political run fades in the history books.

"Dan, what does that have to do with me being winsome?" Glad you asked. In our house, on Sundays, we would work hard to have a dinner where everyone would get asked the question; "What is the best thing that happened to you this week?" We'd celebrate each win, thrill, award, compliment, and special memory.

Importantly, as a family, we'd ask, "What's the toughest thing of your week?" Then, we'd pray for the collection of challenges at the end of the meal.

The power of prayer is greater than even the power of a winsome way. A winsome word, spoken at a special time, can change a life. A prayer, lifted up at just the right time, can change history. Ask David when he met Goliath. Moses when he was at the Red Sea, or who knows, maybe Kurt Warner in his miracle Super Bowl season of 1999 to 2000 and his Super Bowl MVP. *Sports Illustrated* had put Warner on the cover with the title, "Who is this guy?" Warner, I know would say "God knew", as Warner's faith and prayer life were and still are a part of his testimony. As we wind down this sidebar on prayer, it may become for many of you not a sidebar, but a giant part of the relationships you have with your own Winsome Seven.

My Sunday first day of the week 'Winsome' connection is with my children. They are now all out of home and experiencing lives of their own. We can only trust that a moment of encouragement, listening, nurturing, or prayer will echo down the line over time.

WINSOME SEVEN MONDAY:

Monday might be one of the toughest days ever. Jokes are made of Monday. Posters and Twitter feeds opine about Mondays. I do like the hashtag touting #MotivationalMondays that now pepper social media. In general, Americans do not like Monday. But *you* can! Because when you're walking winsome, every day is going to hold something good, and often unexpectedly good!

Choosing your Monday 'winsome' person is important. I call my friend of 40 years, Larry "Bernie" Austin. I wrote of him early on. He is today all the good things I wrote of in opening chapters. For 40 years, he has been a 'go-to' listener and encourager. Bigger than that, we know we are each other's listener and encourager. I'll call 'Bernie' and tell him he's a world-changer through his work with pastors across the Midwest. He'll tell me I am the next Zig Ziglar. Perhaps we may both fall short of those heightened words, yet we each hear a person on a Monday who we know has our back, is our wingman, will cheer us on, and, yes, pick us up when needed. We have walked through great moments and down moments. You must have a true long-term friend for Mondays, because they've seen your great Mondays and awful Mondays and measure you the same. Your Monday winsome team member will help you set the week and remind you of the best and brightest of your days. And most importantly, you will lift them up and ask what you can do to serve them this week.

WINSOME SEVEN TUESDAY:

Michael Saubert, Sr. is my Tuesday winsome guy. All the way. I remember the winsome moment he walked up to me at a Drake University football game. Our sons played together there. My son, Lee, was a year older, and both young men were tight ends. Mike said, "Hey, I want to thank you for your son's mentoring and friendship to our son, Eric." I now can smile, as Mike's son, Eric, now plays pro football in the NFL for the Atlanta Falcons, so my son, Lee, can take maybe one percent credit or some amount. They bonded early. Mike and I bonded as well. A by-chance connection created a winsome life connection. Mike's wife Kim shared a love of photography that I had. Ironically, through that love of picture-taking, I got to be the sideline photographer for the team. I was able to up close and, in the action, so to speak, capturing some great shots of our sons and over a hundred different players who, even to this day, use my pictures as their social media pics. That service which came with no money to me, came from the winsome way thinking of, "Serve others and watch what happens."

Each of us encounters a person we admire or feel a special connection to. Mike always offers an encouraging word, a positive outlook, and a 'can-do' spirit. From our friendship, Mike and I started a video podcast series to encourage other people online and in workshops, called "The Positivity Experience". Imagine, from Chicago to Kansas City, probably never to meet, if not for Coach Chris Creighton (who was previously noted as an 'Enroller') would have seen something in our sons that would be a difference-maker. Those boys shared championship rings and a friendship. From that, two men talk every Tuesday to encourage and be accountability buddies.

WINSOME SEVEN WEDNESDAY:

Winsome Wednesday! A day that you should find a person who you know will challenge you. And you will challenge them. In a good and positive way. We need a challenger in our life. Someone who believes in us, but does not allow us to rest on our laurels. And we don't want them to rest, either. Remember the acronym of WINSOME, a Wednesday Winsome partnership helps especially with being the "M" for Mindful. We challenge one another to be mindful of our talents. Right smack in the middle of the week, we need to be mindful of our talents and remind the other of their giftedness.

My Winsome Wednesday guy is Dr. Randy Shepard. Randy holds a PhD in family studies and was the founder of one of the largest churches in Lee's Summit, Missouri. Randy holds substantial business experience. He has authored two books and has spoken across the globe. I can count on Randy to tell me what I *need* to hear, not what I *want* to hear. He knows I will remind him of his accomplishments, and I also give him ideas that often he turns into bigger gains then either of us could imagine. That's a Wednesday Winsome person key. Get someone who will kick up ideas and energy for ideas that will soar ahead. I call Randy, and we joke about winsomeness and what could be done with it. I think that he and I will develop ideas around the very winsome way concept that even I couldn't have imagined. That's a winsome way friendship and champion.

WINSOME SEVEN THURSDAY:

The now popular phrase 'Throwback Thursday' comes into play for my Thursday person—actually, a couple. Larry and Lauriann Scott, of Lincoln, Nebraska. Yes, the same gas-station-owner-turned-millionaire I worked for and wrote of from my college days. Larry's lasting legacy memory of running out to the cars at the gas pumps is one I speak of often. He showed me whatever the job at hand, do it with gusto and enthusiasm. So why wouldn't I call a guy like that every Thursday? I remind Larry of the incredible motivator he was. Now in his 70s and, perhaps, forgotten by many, I think it important to share with him my appreciation and love of his spirit. He always has a laugh, story, and kind word. I remind him of a funny moment. We talk about Nebraska football and Lincoln. It takes us both back for our time on the phone. It keeps us young. Being winsome is also being young at heart and having a child-like love of people and great moments. Lauriann often is in the background and adds a story or two. Their marriage is a testimony to a husband and wife who stuck together to create an incredible business, family, and friendships.

For your Winsome Thursday person, I suggest a 'throwback' to someone of long ago who helped shape your life. It could be a coach, a manager, a minister, or an employer, like Larry; just someone who you want to reconnect with and finish life encouraging one another.

WINSOME SEVEN FRIDAY:

America has a love affair with Fridays. More enthusiasm for a day surround this day than any other. So, perhaps it should be important that this day holds your most inspiring person.

My Friday call takes me south, to Texas. Two men hold my Friday Winsome connection. I call them the Winsome Texas boys. They are a dynamic duo. Bob Beaudine and Tom Ziglar. You've read of Bob throughout this book. Tom Ziglar, the son of the late Zig Ziglar, carries on the tradition his motivational father set, as he now runs Ziglar, Inc. Tom authored his first book *Choose to Win* in 2018, and like his father, Zig, is changing lives. One incredibly winsome thing that Tom does is when he travels is that he gives the flight crew the gift of the small Zig Ziglar quote books. Tom lights up the skies and leaves a winsome memory in that, for sure! Tom carries on the Ziglar legacy, along with his sisters, Julie Ziglar Norman and Cindy Ziglar Oates. These guys, Bob and Tom, are busy gentlemen. Some Fridays I know I won't catch but one of them. Friday is an important day as you launch into the weekend, so I suggest that it is potentially important that you have two people to try to reach, to make sure you are headed upward. Sometimes, I reach them both. That's a double shot of adrenalin, for sure! These guys are full of so much energy, ideas, inspiration, and excitement, I just try to reflect back half what they send out. It's kind of like playing tennis with a very good player. You can volley with them and, eventually, you know you are playing with a champion. Bob and Tom are true champions. They lift up thousands of people each year through their speaking, podcasts, messages, and social media posts. For each of you, if you're not following Bob and Tom, look them up. You'll be inspired and thankful you did.

As you know, Tom Ziglar's family has had a powerful impact on my life. Zig Ziglar was a key inspiration in the writing of this book, as he encouraged me—as he had many people—to, "Share your good message, so as to help others." His mom, Jean, who joined Zig in Heaven in 2018, was also the inspiration behind the inspiration. At Jean's funeral at the packed Prestonwood Church in Plano, Texas, which I made sure not to miss because of who they were in my life, the theme of the funeral spoke to the winsomeness of Jean… she gave Zig her all in love, support, nurturing, and everything. They were a priceless couple.

Bob' latest book, *2 Chairs* holds a winsome message for sure. After you have finished reading this, off to Amazon or Barnes and Noble you should go for *2 Chairs*. And if you ever connect with Bob, tell him his winsome buddy 'Danny' sent you!

WINSOME SEVEN SATURDAY:

Saturdays often allow us a special extra time to visit with a winsome connection, so this one takes a little time. I suggest another lifelong winsome connection.

My incredible winsome Saturday guy is Gary Novotny. Like many on my Winsome Seven list, I wrote of Gary in my winsome stories. I helped cheer Gary on to become the 2016 Nebraska Retailer of the Year. Then, he went on to the nationals and finished as the fifth ranked in the nation. Gary earned that because he pours his winsome manner into his customers and acquaintances. There is not a Saturday that somehow, we don't connect. Gary and I can relive high school, college, or even adult memories, and always laugh. We often have ideas or encouragement that becomes a fruitful endeavor. In 2020, we will be launching 'Winsome Communities'. Gary will be a part of that speaking and promotional endeavor. If you are a 'Small Town USA' that wants to bring motivational life principles, business, and retail ideas, fundraising, and inspiration to your community, and you're reading this now, I suggest you write us today.

So that's it. My Winsome Seven. Now, how about you? On the next page, you might write down a list of people to think through. People from your past and present. People who you consider inspirational and encouraging. People, couples, or groups of people who you can pour yourself into and also know they'll care about you.

This is where the next 21 days will change you. You will begin daily walking and talking in a more winsome way. You'll be thinking in a different way. You'll be looking for good. You'll be looking for stories, quotes, and inspiration to pass along. The Winsome Way will take life within you.

You wake up every morning with a choice.

You can be Winsome. Or you can be Woesome.

Choose Winsome.

WINSOME SEVEN CANDIDATES

WINSOME SEVEN SELECTIONS

SUNDAY _____

MONDAY _____

TUESDAY _____

WEDNESDAY _____

THURSDAY _____

FRIDAY _____

SATURDAY _____

CHAPTER 11
WINSOME COACHING

A Winsome Conclusion

The "Now What Do We Do?" Question

If you are a Robert Redford fan, as I am, this will flash back with a smile. Since his role as the 'Sundance Kid' in *Butch Cassidy and the Sundance Kid* in 1969, most would agree that Redford has a personal charm and good looks that rocks women and brings the envy of most men. If I looked like Robert Redford or had his twinkling smile, I am sure that book sales would triple wherever I went. Granted, I've disagreed with a few of his political views in recent years, yet we still have to respect a true 'Master of His Craft'. Redford is that. Acting. Directing. Producing.

In 1972 ,he started as Bill McKay in the movie *The Candidate*. I recommend this movie for anyone running for public office at any level. The message I took from the movie was that you will shine brightest and gain favor if you are just being yourself and standing for what you believe. Glean from that thought that also, you will be your most winsome self if you walk in a positive way because you know your heart, strengths, and spirit.

In this movie, though the world of political consultants drove him hard to be something other than himself. I've been in elected office, and have been campaign chairman for gubernatorial, presidential, state, and local elections, so I understand that data, polls, and techniques can drive results. Redford's character had been Governor of California and old school politics was part of the education of the candidate, Bill McKay. They did make him adapt, sometimes against his natural instincts. But McKay rose up and did best when they let his personality, wit, and charm shine. He was coached, just as I have done some of in this book, but in the end, the moments after his election victory, Redford is seen trying over and over to reach and engage his campaign chairman with a very important question. Redford grabs him and quickly goes behind a door and asks the movie-ending question… "Now what do we do?"

Well, you've just won your election. You elected to read this book, *The Winsome Way*, so you might rise up and be even better than you've ever been. It's also fair to ask me, "Dan, now what do I do?"

The answer to that is the same one I told young basketball players for the 20+ years I volunteered as a youth coach at many levels. My message: 'Practice. Repeat. Practice, and do it with heart!"

Repetition in anything takes the uncomfortable to comfortable. I would encourage in practices…

> *"Repetition, Repetition, Repetition! What you do in practice you will do in the game!"*

What you do in practice you will do in the game. It's so true. Living, walking, and being winsome holds the same message. Developing an attitude of "I am winsome at home, at work, on the street, whatever the situation," will allow you to truly shine.

And it will take practice. As we talked about in the "M" for 'Be Mindful' chapter, the old adage of "I can't change" doesn't hold true. Remember your first basketball, volleyball, football, baseball, or sports practice? Could you do a layup very easy your first time? Could you shoot a free throw without practice and practice? How about learning to play the piano or another instrument? The 'getting good at it' part of your sports skill or any talent, for that matter, came about after practice, practice,

practice. Then, it became natural. Being winsome is not unlike riding a bicycle or making chocolate chip cookies. You can do it! Once you learn it and become steady, you'll never forget how, just like when you learned to ride that bike. Now, today, you will learn to walk winsomely into a room or any situation and roll down the street successfully.

Importantly in the "Now what do we do?" question, I am happy to say I am as WINSOME for you now as the day you purchased this book. I'm Willing, Interested, want to Nurture you, help be your Solutioneer, have us be Optimistic together, as well as Mindful. And, then, together, Enroll you in a brighter future!

To that extent, I will offer a series of three months of monthly live webinars, at no cost, via live broadcast tools that are interactive, where you can ask questions, share stories, and maybe be highlighted as a 'Winsome Wonder'. You invested in me by purchasing this book. I want to give back. So right now, set down this book… get your email going and send me a quick note to Dan@TheWinsomeWay.com, and I'll send you the invite to the enrollment page for the monthly live book discussion of *The Winsome Way*.

At our website TheWinsomeWay.com, we offer multiple levels of personal, professional, and business coaching. The Winsome Way Coaching Systems have teamed with Dr. Randy Shepard, noted national tax expert; and Michael Saubert, Sr., who has led the design team for Craftsman tools, Kenmore appliances, and most of the noted historic success at Sears for the last 20+ years. We have a comprehensive Business Startup Coaching Program to help launch your ideas and dreams. Alongside these programs' workshops, seminars, and webinars.

- Winsome Summits – an inspirational weekend with speakers in a high-energy atmosphere

- Winsome in a Week – group walk through the concepts interactively and with interaction and Q&A

- One-on-One Intensive Winsome Coaching

- Group Call Winsome Coaching

- Building Your Winsome Life

- Dream, Design, and Do It – a multi-coach business design and coaching program

I can't wait to hear from you, meet you, or see you shine! Until then, stay WINSOME, my friend!

ABOUT THE AUTHOR

'America's Winsomeologist'

DAN SNELL

has walked and shared a journey of success as well as encouraging others toward their dreams and goals. Snell's life of looking for the good in each person, and in every day and life situation via a 'see others first' outlook has garnered him great success and a lifelong legacy of personal and business relationships that echo throughout the world.

Dan Snell grew up in small town USA. That Nebraska, heartland of America, upbringing set the foundation for the spirit, outlook and 'can do' attitude that today brings forth this winsome way message.

Snell has achieved success in the world of business, sports, politics, public speaking and ministry. His interest in public service led him to be active in politics and community service for the last 30+ years. Along that journey he's met and shaken hands with five US Presidents, held elective political office for 10 years, developed leadership and economic development programs. He also served to lead campaigns for other winning candidates. Dan understands and believes what true 'winsome' public service is about and has lived that out and taught that successfully.

Professionally, Snell garnered top awards in sales and management. Earning over 10 President's Clubs for top achievers, once being awarded the 'Best of the Best' in healthcare sales at Kronos, his unique, enthusiastic and winsome style helped all around him succeed. Dan understands and carries a clear understanding of the energy, creativity and the 'work smart' style that it takes to win the day and be a true champion in sales and sales management.

Snell's faith stands as a foundation for many of his life principles. The experiences and fruit of those beliefs inspired Snell to speak at major men's, family and fathering conferences. He was the co-founder of a national ministry to serve stepfamilies, the largest family demographic in America today. Dan co-hosted the 'first-of-it's-kind' ever national radio programto stepfamilies, called 'Blended Family Today'.

His love of athletics took him into the world of professional sports in the 80's, as Snell was selected to be part of the NBA referee development program and officiated in the CBA, the then minor leagues for the NBA. Today Snell serves and is active in the Small College Basketball Hall of Fame. He has coached youth sports for over 30 years.

Snell has three grown children, Sarah, Lee and Amanda. All carry a winsome spirit in their own lives.

www.ingramcontent.com/pod-product-compliance
Lightning Source LLC
LaVergne TN
LVHW012210070526
838202LV00027B/2634/J